The Complete Guide to Selling and Marketing to Affluent Customers

Everything You Need to Know
to Attract and Keep Wealthy Customers

Tamsen Butler

THE COMPLETE GUIDE TO SELLING AND MARKETING TO AFFLUENT CUSTOMERS: EVERYTHING YOU NEED TO KNOW TO ATTRACT AND KEEP WEALTHY CUSTOMERS

Library of Congress Cataloging-in-Publication Data

Butler, Tamsen, 1974-
The complete guide to selling and marketing to affluent customers : everything you need to know to attract and keep wealthy customers / Tamsen Butler.
p. cm.
Includes bibliographical references and index.
ISBN-13: 978-1-60138-327-3 (alk. paper)
ISBN-10: 1-60138-327-4 (alk. paper)
1. Affluent consumers. 2. Consumer behavior. 3. Marketing. 4. Selling. I. Title.
HF5415.332.A34B88 2011
658.8--dc23
2011022357

Printed in the United States

Printed on Recycled Paper

INTERIOR LAYOUT: Antoinette D'Amore • addesign@videotron.ca
COVER DESIGN: Jackie Miller • sullmill@charter.net

A few years back we lost our beloved pet dog Bear, who was not only our best and dearest friend but also the "Vice President of Sunshine" here at Atlantic Publishing. He did not receive a salary but worked tirelessly 24 hours a day to please his parents.

Bear was a rescue dog who turned around and showered myself, my wife, Sherri, his grandparents Jean, Bob, and Nancy, and every person and animal he met (well, maybe not rabbits) with friendship and love. He made a lot of people smile every day.

We wanted you to know a portion of the profits of this book will be donated in Bear's memory to local animal shelters, parks, conservation organizations, and other individuals and nonprofit organizations in need of assistance.

– *Douglas & Sherri Brown*

PS: We have since adopted two more rescue dogs: first Scout, and the following year, Ginger. They were both mixed golden retrievers who needed a home.

Want to help animals and the world? Here are a dozen easy suggestions you and your family can implement today:

- *Adopt and rescue a pet from a local shelter.*
- *Support local and no-kill animal shelters.*
- *Plant a tree to honor someone you love.*
- *Be a developer — put up some birdhouses.*
- *Buy live, potted Christmas trees and replant them.*
- *Make sure you spend time with your animals each day.*
- *Save natural resources by recycling and buying recycled products.*
- *Drink tap water, or filter your own water at home.*
- *Whenever possible, limit your use of or do not use pesticides.*
- *If you eat seafood, make sustainable choices.*
- *Support your local farmers market.*
- *Get outside. Visit a park, volunteer, walk your dog, or ride your bike.*

Five years ago, Atlantic Publishing signed the Green Press Initiative. These guidelines promote environmentally friendly practices, such as using recycled stock and vegetable-based inks, avoiding waste, choosing energy-efficient resources, and promoting a no-pulping policy. We now use 100-percent recycled stock on all our books. The results: in one year, switching to post-consumer recycled stock saved 24 mature trees, 5,000 gallons of water, the equivalent of the total energy used for one home in a year, and the equivalent of the greenhouse gases from one car driven for a year.

Dedication

For my big brother Josh Matthies and his adorable kiddos, Ava, Nicky, and Fuzzy.

Table of Contents

Introduction

Joseph Aisenson is CEO and president of Delta Mechanical in the affluent Southern California community of Calabasas. Not only is he frequently targeted as an individual consumer, he is also enthusiastically courted by companies that want to sell him goods and services for his thriving business. He has grown accustomed to the marketing tactics he now expects when a salesperson shows up at his business. Gifts, trips, and meals at swanky restaurants are all par for the course.

"Salesmen take my wife and me to dinner at nice restaurants quite frequently," Aisenson said. "They try really hard to get to know me and to make sure that my staff knows who they are. It is true that this type of treatment makes me notice them, and maybe I will take their call quicker than if I had no idea who they were, but the truth is that it always comes down to who can offer me the best product at the best price. They can pay for my dinner, and they can send me gifts, but I am a businessman, and I make my decisions based on what is best for my business."

There is much more to marketing to affluent customers than buying a couple of dinners or getting a customer's attention by sending a few gifts. Although you can be sure that affluent customers will expect to be treated well — exceptionally well, as a matter of fact — it is usually not enough to rely on schmoozing to get these customers to open their wallets. You have to offer a product they want at a price they are willing to pay.

The question then becomes how to get affluent customers to want what you are selling and agree to pay the price you command. Start by throwing your preconceptions about this class of customers out the window; they are a varied bunch and cannot be easily lumped into one single predictable group. Not all affluent people drive luxury vehicles, and not all affluent people carry wallets packed with American Express "black cards." The boisterous woman who marches into your boutique wearing a designer dress and an expensive watch might be on the verge of bankruptcy, while the modestly dressed man who does not command attention might have millions of dollars sitting in his bank account.

How do you get the attention of the customers who have the financial means to pay for your product or service? You have to know who you are marketing to and what your target market looks for. You have to understand how the affluent mind works. You have to build an impeccable reputation and make a name for your product or service. Marketing to affluent customers includes creating a desire for your product or service and making that desire strong enough to prompt the customer to act. Perhaps most importantly, you have to offer affluent customers a service or product they actually want to pay for. If you can offer something that these customers will actually be attracted to — whether it is luxury vehicles, premium chocolates, or a tailoring service — you can benefit from concentrating your marketing and selling efforts onto this particular group.

Here is the good news: If you can obtain and keep wealthy individuals as a customer base, then you are poised to succeed. This book gives the information you need to successfully market to affluent customers by delving into the way affluent customers think, the way they make their purchases, and what works, as well as what does not work, when trying to get the attention of the wealthy. Everything you learn will help you to better understand your desired customer and increase your chances of joining their ranks as a result of your own success.

Chapter 1

The Inclinations of Affluent Customers

> *"Don't judge men's wealth or godliness by their Sunday appearance."*
>
> Benjamin Franklin, Founding Father and famous inventor

The affluent customer base is an interesting market to target. If you can get the affluent interested in what you are selling, people who are not able to boast affluent status will take notice of what the affluent are buying and, as a result, want to buy those same products. Other consumers take notice of what affluent people drive, what they wear, where they shop, and where they go on vacation. Affluent people live a lifestyle that many other consumers wish they could live, and if the average consumer cannot afford to live the affluent lifestyle, maybe he or she can mimic it.

For this reason, successfully marketing to affluent customers opens up doors to other customer bases you might not have even considered. An affluent customer might buy an ostentatious bracelet to wear at a special event and wind up photographed wearing it. Then, other people take notice and want the same bracelet — even if it means buying one on credit. The bracelet might be beautiful, but it also represents prosperity, status, and the ability to acquire beautiful things.

By attracting affluent customers to your product or service, your options for becoming a financially successful businessperson increase exponentially.

Wealth Powers the Train — as do Wealthy Customers

Affluent customers are the movers and the shakers when it comes to prompting people to want to buy goods and services. Affluent neighborhoods are repeatedly mimicked on a smaller scale; middle-class neighborhoods are sprinkled with luxury cars and occasional visits from cleaning services. Even communities with modest financial means occasionally might show a penchant for expensive products.

The buying power of the wealthy

Affluent people do not have to labor over most purchasing decisions like many other customers do, but this does not mean all affluent people will make purchase decisions on a whim and without any regard for cost or quality. Simply put, even the most affluent customers can find themselves losing that wealthy status fairly quickly if they routinely run amok with their money, spending with reckless abandon without considering the bigger financial picture. Consider the celebrities, athletes, and lottery winners who go from being mega-millionaires to being millions of dollars in debt before the public's eye. All affluent people run the risk of winding up in bankruptcy if they are not careful, even if the media spotlight is not focused on them.

The most powerful customers are those who are affluent but also discerning and meticulous. They often do not spend their money frivolously and instead buy things because they have made the decision that they want these things. Simply put, these customers have money to spend, and if you can compel them to want to buy your product or service, you will make money.

Products

What type of products do affluent customers buy? You can typically expect affluent customers to want luxurious items, but not all affluent customers buy these items with the sole intention of showing off their wealth. Instead, they can afford and have experienced luxuries, and as a result, they want luxury.

The process of buying a car is a good example. These consumers will look for luxury but also state-of-the-art safety features, as well as bells and whistles that will make their driving experience more enjoyable. It is usually not enough to market a car as flashy or fast. These customers expect their vehicles to proactively avoid collisions, such as the Mercedes® Attention Assist feature that senses when the driver is falling asleep. They expect the systems in their vehicles to constantly monitor the stability of the car, as in the Porsche® Stability Management system. They assume the car they buy will have active safety systems, including stability control, traction control, and anti-lock brake systems, the features seen in Aston Martin vehicles. Their cars should be able to tell them how to get from one side of town to another, call for help if the driver becomes unconscious, and provide the smoothest ride possible, all while looking stylish.

You will notice that affluent customers *expect* these features as opposed to simply *wanting* them. Compelling affluent customers to purchase something that does not have all the expected features will prove to be quite difficult. People who have enough money to demand the best will be incredibly reluctant to settle for anything less.

If you do not have the product an affluent customer wants, there is a good chance he or she will go elsewhere unless or until you can prove what you have is better. By trying to convince affluent customers that extras such as state-of-the-art safety features are unnecessary, you are not only marketing incredibly ineffectively, you might wind up insulting them. A golden rule of marketing to the affluent is this: Do not offend your customers.

Services

At a roadside fast-food establishment, you probably do not expect to have the best customer service you have ever experienced, but when you walk into a five-star restaurant, your expectations are much higher. You should be greeted by name and your jacket should be taken. You should not have to wait for your table, the staff should be courteous and swift, and the food and drinks should be impeccably pleasing.

What is the difference between the fast-food place and the luxury restaurant? The expectations are different. One eatery is marketed as a quick place to grab an inexpensive meal while the other is marketed as an elegant dining experience. Simply put, if you market your service as a luxury, you better provide a luxurious experience.

Wealthy customers do not only purchase luxury services. They need their washing machines repaired and tires rotated like everyone else. So, how do they choose the service provider with which to spend their money? Some mega-affluent customers do not make these decisions; their staffs make them, but for affluent customers who make these decisions for themselves, they base their choices on factors such as:

- **Cost:** Do not assume that merely marketing services as prestigious and expensive will have affluent customers flocking to your business. The average wealthy customer is wealthy as a result of careful financial planning, and for this reason, these customers are acutely aware of the cost of the services they purchase. The money you charge for your services should be comparable to what other service providers offer within your area. Charge more if you offer additional services — and you should offer additional services if you hope to attract affluent customers — but do not make the mistake of thinking a higher price tag will somehow subliminally attract affluent customers to your business. You should be able to confidently finish this sentence: "We charge a little more for our services because we also offer … ." How do you justify the additional costs? Is your customer service impeccable? Is your company the highest rated in the region in customer satisfaction? If you plan to charge more, be prepared to justify why. An affluent customer using your services will require justification before he or she visits your establishment.

- **Reputation:** Affluent customers will not only refuse to return to a service provider who does not provide adequate services, but they also will tell other people about their experiences. Even if customers do not directly tell you that they are unhappy, chances are good that word will spread. Customers remember what their friends and colleagues say about service providers and will make purchase decisions based on the anecdotes they hear. Your primary concern should be to make sure the main service you provide is the best around. Additional luxury services should be secondary concerns. For example, if you offer car detailing services and do a lousy job detailing the vehicle, do you really think that offering courtesy pickup services for vehicles is going to cancel out the fact that the primary service you offer is not up to par? Such a huge portion of marketing is the impression you make on your customers and the word-of-mouth recommendations that spread as a result. Consider this more valuable than any other form of marketing, and act accordingly by making sure the services you offer are phenomenal.

- **Responses:** How do you respond to affluent customers? If a wealthy customer asks for a service you typically do not provide, do you automatically deny the request, or do you make every effort to fulfill it? Suppose a dog walker in an affluent neighborhood is asked by a client to once a week give the family dog a bath after a walk. The dog walker can either say, "No, sorry, I am not a groomer," or figure out a way to make it happen. A smart entrepreneur will immediately recognize this as a viable need, and he or she will make the educated assumption that it must be a need for other customers in the neighborhood. The smart dog walker will either give the dog a bath or align with a groomer to make it happen. Ideally, word will spread that the neighborhood dog walker responds quickly to requests, and the customer base for the dog walker will expand. What does the dog walker in an affluent neighborhood have to do with services you provide? This dog walker listens to customer requests and quickly responds, thereby marketing himself or herself as the type of dog walker residents want. This dog walker becomes the "it" dog walker, just as you want to become the "it" service provider in your niche.

Therefore, it is not enough to merely offer luxury services. You have to offer services that affluent customers need and want, as well as offer them in an excellent way. Never underestimate the power of a job well done because word-of-mouth marketing is incredibly potent, particularly among an affluent customer base.

CASE STUDY: WORD OF SHODDY SERVICE SPREADS QUICKLY

Heide
Stay-at-home mom

When Heide's second baby was born, she brought in some help to keep the house clean. Living in an affluent neighborhood in Omaha, Nebraska, she had her choice of several housecleaning services because these services were aggressively marketed in particular toward her neighborhood.

"I hired a service I had seen ads for. It was a national company that sent teams of cleaners to the house in a company car; everyone was supposed to have insurance, a background check, and all those things, so it seemed to me that this would be the way to go instead of hiring one person to do the job," Heide said. After the first cleaning, she had complaints that the high chair was not moved in order to clean the floor underneath. When she pointed this out to the cleaning crew, they were not receptive to her complaint, and when it happened a second time at the next scheduled cleaning, Heide promptly canceled the service.

The story does not end there. It just so happened that Heide was quite active with a large group of other stay-at-home mothers from other affluent neighborhoods within the city and surrounding areas. While hosting a playdate at her home, she retold the story to all the mothers, many of whom were also considering hiring a cleaning service. Not one single mother from this group hired the cleaning company Heide had used as a direct result of the experience she had shared during the playdate, and many of these mothers retold the story to friends of theirs. Stay-at-home mothers in affluent neighborhoods are well connected with each other, and they are commonly the ones within the home who make the decisions regarding which services to hire. In this instance, a less-than-impressive cleaning crew resulted in several potential customers adopting a negative attitude toward the cleaning company.

What would have happened if the cleaning crew had immediately fixed the problem or, better yet, there had been no problem to begin with? "I would have told my friends about the cleaning service in a positive way," Heide said. "They would have gotten a lot of business from my friends."

The buying habits of the wealthy

Research shows that the buying habits of the wealthy fluctuate with the economy, even if the affluent customers are largely unaffected by economic fluctuations. For example, an October 2010 article in *The Economist* stated that many affluent customers backed off luxury purchases during the Great Recession, which began December 2007, even when they could still afford to make the purchases. Whether they held off on the purchases for of fear of future financial difficulties or appearing ostentatious while other people were struggling, many affluent customers simply made the decision not to pursue luxury purchases or to wait until the items they wanted went on sale. Customers who did make purchases sometimes asked for items to be wrapped in plain bags instead of bags featuring the logo of the luxury product because they did not want to appear pretentious.

Of course, this is not true for all affluent customers. Some wealthy customers continue buying vacation homes and diamond necklaces despite an economic downturn and do not try to hide their purchases. Remember, affluent customers are a diverse base of individuals. Although the majority of wealthy customers might respond in one way, there is always bound to be a deviation from the norm.

Affluent customers have an advantage over other consumers because they can afford to indulge in things they want. Although some affluent customers might be careful in their spending, clipping coupons and hunting down sales, they might also be willing to shell out shockingly large amounts of money for the things they really want. An affluent customer might balk at designer clothing and live in a middle-class neighborhood, but when it comes to the customer's true passion, the money flows freely. Whether it is travel to exotic places, showering grandchildren with expensive gifts, or purchasing the best wine money can buy, if you can get the attention of wealthy consumers who are passionate about your product, you can make quite a bit of money. Customers who want these products might call you instead of you calling them, and they will already be eager to make the purchase. The key when looking at this phenomenon is marketing your item or service as something an affluent customer can be passionate about. Study the enthusiasts of your product or service, or better yet, create enthusiasm for your service or product by making it something amazing and enjoyable.

Quality over quantity

Not all affluent customers are concerned about appearing affluent, though most affluent customers are quite concerned about the quality of the items they purchase. There is a huge difference between quality and quantity. For example, an affluent customer will probably be more inclined to purchase a diamond ring that has one amazing diamond on the band than he or she would be to buy a ring with a cluster of similar-sized diamonds that are of poor clarity and color. It might not even matter to this customer whether other people realize that the lone diamond is more expensive than a cluster of similarly sized diamonds of a lesser value; this customer knows, which is what is important.

It is difficult to go back to poor-quality products after you have experienced the luxuries money can buy. Think of it in these terms: Suppose you buy two hot dogs for $2 that taste a little weird and give you indigestion. The next day, you buy one hot dog from a competing hot dog cart for $5, and it tastes fantastic, and upon inquiring as to why the hot dog does not give you indigestion, you are told that it is all natural. The next time you want a hot dog and have $5 to spend, which hot dog will you buy? In terms of marketing to an affluent customer base, you want to let your customers know that you sell the $5 hot dogs.

Money can buy clothing that does not fade, blankets that do not itch, airline tickets that do not include long lines at the gate, and homes in neighborhoods where crime is virtually unheard of. Customers who have the money necessary to experience these items and services will probably have a difficult time accepting anything other than these luxuries because they know they have the money to buy the best. Keep the importance of quality over quantity in mind while planning a marketing strategy. Quantity might appeal to some target markets, but if your hope is to tap into the affluent customer market, you need to use marketing tactics that enhance knowledge of the quality of the products or services you offer.

About Your Customers

Affluent customers will buy in bulk for basic things they need, such as groceries or toiletries, but do not expect them to concern themselves with quantity when buying high-priced items.

Demands for levels of service

Although it is true that affluent customers do generally expect a higher level of service, the range of demands can vary wildly. One affluent customer might be completely thrilled by having a dedicated shopping assistant when visiting a store and consider this exceptional customer service. Another customer might only be impressed by businesses with a uniformed door attendant, a dedicated shopping assistant who also happens to know the customer's name and personal shopping preferences, champagne while trying on clothing, another assistant to run out and grab lunch for the customer, and prompt and courteous delivery of all purchased items to the customer's front door. The level of service an affluent customer will expect generally depends on two factors:

1. The level of service the affluent customer has experienced in the past

2. The personality of the affluent customer

Never scale back on the level of service you provide. If customers have grown accustomed to having a cup of steaming chamomile tea handed to them upon arrival at your boutique, suddenly halting the tea service will not go over well with your customers. The underlying assumption by most affluent customers will be that you are cutting financial corners for one reason or another, whether it is because your business is hurting financially or you have decided you do not need to take care of your customers. Either way, decisions like these are bad news for your business.

Affluent customers naturally assume that if they are going to put hundreds or thousands of dollars in your pocket, you should treat them quite well. This is true to a certain extent; however, you certainly do not want to force your staff to submit to every whim of your customers. Staff members should not have to endure belittling and abuse just to get a sale, but they should be willing to do whatever reasonable things need to be done in order to make an affluent customer feel welcome and valued.

Be prepared to offer service beyond what is traditionally offered. This is what affluent customers expect, and those who do not expect it will probably like the service and be more likely to return. Repeat business will be the key to keeping your business thriving, particularly when affluent customers are your focus.

Creatures of habit

When affluent customers find a product or service they like or trust, there is an excellent chance they will stick with it. In an economic slump, other customers might be more willing to seek out cheaper alternatives to the items they typically buy than affluent customers. Affluent customers are generally regarded by marketing professionals as more "brand loyal" than other customers. Almost as important is that these customers will likely tell their acquaintances about the product or service or will be seen with the product or using the service.

If you can keep affluent customers happy, it increases the odds of repeat business the next time they need something else you offer, but you cannot rely on this as your main marketing tactic. Remember that affluent customers are constantly being courted by other people who want to sell them goods or services. Depending on affluent customers to be merely creatures of habit minimizes the need to keep these customers happy and satisfied and will thus leave you open to the risk of those customers finding something bigger and better next time.

You can purchase many different types of complex computer programs to analyze your customers' loyalty to your brand, but if you run a small business, these programs are probably not financially reasonable. You do not need computer software to tell you whether your customers are loyal to your business; you just need to pay attention to whether they keep coming back.

The Buying Habits of Regular Customers

The buying habits of nonaffluent customers can be difficult trends to analyze for a variety of reasons. Many customers have delved into more affluent purchasing patterns as a result of increased exposure — courtesy of the Internet and other media outlets — to the finer things in life. This is why a homemaker in the Midwest might walk into a boutique and slap an already-near-maxed-out credit card down on the counter to purchase a pair of expensive designer shoes or a handbag that is typically reserved for people with a much higher annual incomes. This is also why some teenagers without jobs still expect to have all of the latest technologies regardless of cost. The mystery of luxury items is gone. People who might have otherwise never heard of Prada or Maybach before can now see these items regularly via the television or the Internet.

As a direct result, customers who do not necessarily qualify as affluent might still expect to someday purchase luxury items and will also expect to be treated as affluent when doing so. In other words, do not discount the buying power of the middle class, or even of the lower class, because some of these consumers can and will figure out how to get their hands on luxury items.

Aside from the everyday consumers who aspire to own the things they see their favorite celebrities flaunting, research shows that certain trends can be attributed to consumers as a whole:

- Consumers are becoming less willing to pay full price for items. They search for coupons online before making many of their purchases, both major and routine.

- Consumers pay attention to marketing and do not like covert marketing schemes.

- Consumers will use credit to make purchases they do not necessarily need.

- Consumers pay attention to labels and brands.

- Consumers are incredibly influenced by their peers when making purchasing decisions.

- Consumers are generally willing to pay for convenience.

Why should you care about the behavior of consumers in general if you main focus is affluent customers? Keep in mind that not everyone is born affluent. Many people earn their affluent status after years of hard work and keen financial management, and it is likely these people will retain a good portion of their original consumer behavior.

CASE STUDY: COMMON MISTAKES

Matthew T. Seevers, Ph.D.
Assistant professor of marketing
Creighton University

One of the worst approaches to selling and marketing to affluent customers is to assume that all affluent consumers are insensitive to high prices. Even among the wealthy, price is likely to be a relevant attribute for many of the purchases they make. Wealthy consumers still consider the trade-off between a product's benefits and its associated costs — or by extension, the cost-benefit available from a particular seller. For this reason, affluent consumers still shop at Walmart and Sam's Club.

A related mistake is that sellers might falsely assume affluent consumers always buy the "best in class" product and that less affluent consumers never buy the best. Any individual consumer, regardless of wealth, might be willing spend a disproportionately larger (or smaller) percentage of his or her income for a particular purchase. For example, I might be relatively poor, but I might still buy the most expensive smart phone because perhaps a phone is important in my life or because I desire the status that goes along with ownership of the most luxurious smart phone.

Who are the Wealthy Customers?

Affluent customers are a varied group, which is why it can be so difficult to initially ascertain whether you are actually dealing with an affluent customer or someone who just looks affluent. The other side of the coin is that you might have a customer who appears to most people to be an average consumer, yet has millions of dollars in assets but does not subscribe to an affluent lifestyle.

It is important to understand that the type of affluent customer you are dealing with can usually be directly related to the person's spending behavior. Think about the difference between a customer who has always had unlimited funds at his or her disposal as opposed to another customer who has tirelessly worked for years to get to a point of financial independence. While one customer might think nothing of spending thousands of dollars on a whim, the other might still shudder at the idea of parting with money altogether. Learn the difference between the variety of affluent customers, and you will be better prepared to gauge the willingness of customers to make purchases.

Never forget that not everyone fits into a tidy stereotype. For example, a professional athlete might be fastidious about where he or she spends money, just as a person who comes from years of generational family wealth might decide to shun a luxurious lifestyle. Knowing your customers' backgrounds and how they came into money can certainly be useful when marketing to the affluent, but it is not a fail-safe method for determining how to get people to part with their money.

Defining affluence

When people talk about marketing to the affluent, do they mean people who live in castles in Europe or are they talking about high-paid doctors who are still paying off student loans from medical school? The answer is both. Although an average household income of $100,000 is generally considered affluent within the United States, most companies marketing to affluent customers are trying to catch the attention of households that annually bring in more than $250,000. A lot can depend on the area in which the household is located, as well. For example, the median household income for a family in Ceredo, West Virginia, is less than $30,000, while the median household income for a family in Beverly Hills, California, is nearly three times that amount, according to City-Data.com. A family in Ceredo with an average annual income of $100,000 probably sticks out like a sore thumb as a result of its wealth, while a family in Beverly Hills with an average annual income of $100,000 will likely have some issues staying afloat financially. Affluence is impacted by the location. In some areas of the country a dollar will simply stretch much further.

A further classification of affluent population is the group of people who fall within the subcategory of mega-affluent, which some people consider an appropriate label for people who earn at least $1,000,000 annually. These numbers can be deceiving, however.

Some affluent people might not pull in $1,000,000 per year but have a huge amount of money in assets. Consider people who are retired but have enough money to live an opulent lifestyle with plenty of financial cushion for luxurious purchases. They might not qualify for the classification of mega-affluent because they do not earn $1,000,000 annually, but they certainly have enough money to fit into this category.

The cash poor

Not everyone who is affluent based on income has a lot of money to spare. Some people have so much of their money tied up in real estate, businesses, and other investments that they simply cannot afford to throw their money around and make luxurious purchases. Some people do make quite a bit of money, yet their affluent lifestyle has gotten them into financial trouble. Foreclosure signs do not only show up in poor neighborhoods; affluent people can get in over their heads, too, and wind up owing money to many different sources. These people are in no position to succumb to marketing tactics designed to get them to spend more money.

It is important to realize that not every affluent person can be a customer even if you can manage to market to him or her effectively. Although there are indeed some affluent people who merely need a nudge in order to peak their interest, others cannot be convinced to buy products because they do not have the cash to do so.

It is a different scenario if you extend credit to affluent customers, which allows them to buy your products or services without needing the cash for the purchase. However, when extending credit, great risk is involved. Unless you are willing to use a service to run credit reports to ascertain creditworthiness, you are putting your business at risk. Simply put, do not give a customer your product or service based on a handshake and a promise of payment just because that customer appears affluent. It is one thing to allow customers you are familiar with to pay you later, but it is another to assume that someone has money and agree to a vague future payment.

It is important to be aware of the existence of affluent people who are cash poor. They have huge houses and fancy cars, but they likely owe money for these things. The designer suit a cash poor customer wears might have been bought using a nearly maxed-out credit card. There are also cash poor affluent people who do not necessarily owe money to creditors yet do not have access to their money as a result of their business dealings. The difference between the two is that while one affluent cash-poor customer is heading straight toward bankruptcy, the other cash poor affluent customer is working toward building assets and might come out of the situation with even more money.

Old money versus new money

Some people come from money. Their family has money; therefore, they have money, and there is a chance these people did absolutely nothing to earn their wealth beyond simply being born into privilege. Conversely, there are people who are first genera-tion millionaires who grew up in a different situation, whether it was a middle-class or poor environment. A person's upbringing can potentially affect how he or she spends money, regardless of whether he or she winds up wealthy or impoverished.

It is possible to gain insight into how a wealthy person will spend money based on where the money came from, but if you use ex-cellent marketing and selling techniques, you will have a better chance of enticing affluent customers no matter their background. In other words, know your customers, but do not rely solely on this knowledge to guide your marketing decisions.

It is a relatively safe assumption that people who earn their mon-ey through their own hard work and discipline might be more reluctant to part with it than someone who has unlimited funds thanks to generational wealth. Although this is a fairly reliable trend, it is not carved in stone. You might encounter self-made millionaires who spend money as though it is water, and you might have a customer who comes from years of seemingly un-limited wealth who is apprehensive and meticulous about mak-ing any major purchases. In general, however, you might find that people who have generational wealth — also referred to as "old money" — do not dwell over major purchases as much as people who know what it is like to keep to a careful budget. Af-fluent customers who have always had money simply might not know what it is like to not have money always available.

The importance of money might lose its luster for someone who has never lived without it. On the other hand, a person who is newly affluent might want to compensate for years of not being affluent and might be more apt to spend great amounts of money on a whim.

Although you cannot concretely rely on a person's financial background to reveal who will be more willing to spend larger amounts of money, you can certainly use the knowledge to increase your odds of a sale. Suppose a customer tells you she has just acquired a high-paying job. She is excited about the position and eager to talk about her new role. This is your opportunity to capitalize on the situation. Instead of merely selling her an expensive watch, you are selling her a luxurious item to usher her into this new station in life. Do not merely sell the features of the watch; sell the concept of the customer in her new high-paying position and allow the success to be represented by the watch. Do not say, "You should celebrate your new job by buying this expensive watch." Instead say, "This watch will certainly make a statement about you when you walk into a room." Buying the watch becomes an acceptance of her new role. In psychological terms, this phenomenon is referred to as "transference," but the term you should be concerned about in this situation is "profit."

Suppose another customer walks into your boutique to buy a watch, but this customer is different in that she comes from an affluent family with years of generational wealth. Your approach with her will be different. She probably does not have a psychological desire to buy something that will signify her role in society like your previous customer did. Instead, she wants to buy a watch because she needs a watch, and her affluence just so happens to allow her to stroll into an expensive boutique to buy it. You do not necessarily have to convince this customer she needs the watch, but instead, you need to convince her why she should buy this particular watch.

How are you supposed to know the difference between old money and new money? Salespeople should be trained to talk to customers and find out more about them without being pushy. It is a good idea to ask if a major purchase is for a particular occasion, but often, merely listening to the customer will reveal everything the salesperson needs to know.

When information is not available because a customer is not willing to reveal anything, do not make assumptions about a customer that will influence the way you sell. In other words, just because a woman is not wearing designer shoes does not mean she lacks the financial means to buy whatever she wants. She might come from a family that has been affluent for several generations, and she happens to dislike designer shoes.

High-profile wealthy

There is a special subculture within the affluent population composed of people who are not only wealthy but also well-known because of their celebrity status. These are people you would recognize if they walked into a room, even if you had never personally met them, or people who have names that are brought up in popular culture. Celebrities are an incredibly important group when you are marketing to the affluent for more than one reason.

Not all celebrities have huge bank accounts, yet these people are in the limelight and can compel other people to buy what you sell. For example, a celebrity who wears one of your signature items or drives one of your cars can be worth more than a full-blown ad campaign. People already want to be like celebrities, and because people can only hope to emulate their favorite public figures, one way to do so is by buying the things these celebrities have. People might not even make the connection as to why they want these things; they might not consciously think, "My favorite singer was photographed carrying this handbag," or "That amazing quarterback wore this shirt while being interviewed on my favorite sports show." Their minds take in the information and file it away for later, and then when they have the opportunity to make the purchase, they do so and might not even realize why they feel so urgently led toward the product or service.

The same principle exists for fictional characters, as well. Suppose a character on a well-known television show is seen wearing a certain pair of sunglasses, and these sunglasses are seen by many viewers who either like or identify with the character, perhaps even on a subconscious level. The sunglasses then become a symbol of a way to become like or get closer to the character. The character wears the sunglasses, and the viewers want the sunglasses; thus, another great marketing tactic is successful.

This marketing tactic is known as product placement and involves infusing products into situations where the target market might not necessarily realize that marketing is being presented. Product placement is supposed to be an understated form of advertising because it does not come in the form of blatant advertising. With product placement, consumers often do not realize a product is being advertised to them. In most movies produced today, product placement plays an important role, whether it is the type of soft drink the main character drinks or the type of car that repeatedly shows up throughout the film. Companies pay quite a bit to have their products placed in television shows and films because this has proven to be an effective marketing tactic.

About Your Customers

Track the product placement marketing tactics used in your favorite films by visiting Brandchannel's website at **www.brandchannel.com/brandcameo_films.asp**.

Obviously, there is great benefit to having high-profile celebrity clients, but beyond this, many celebrities have money to burn. Some celebrities pull in more money than they can spend without making some outrageous purchases. You can benefit greatly from these types of clients; they want to spend money, they can spend money, and if they like you and your product, they will probably come back to your business to spend more.

However, you have to be careful when marketing and selling to celebrities. Remember that members of this culture are accustomed to being treated differently than other people, and though you should already provide excellent customer service to all of your customers, it is vital to provide exceptional, superb, one-of-a-kind service to these customers. It is fundamentally true that not one human being is more important than another, but regardless, consider high-profile wealthy customers to be one of the most important segments of your customer population.

You can generally expect high-profile wealthy customers to be trendsetters instead of followers. Marketing the uniqueness of an item or service can be an effective marketing strategy for these people because they want to create trends. These customers might also be more apt to buy expensive items on impulse, so leading them toward an item or service aggressively can be effective in some instances.

CASE STUDY: EFFECTIVENESS OF PRODUCT PLACEMENT

Richard Turke
Director of Ogma Films
Los Angeles, California

Working product placement into a scene can be tricky, but the best directors know how to compel viewers' eyes toward something without the viewers knowing their attention is being pulled in a certain direction. Product placement needs to be put into a natural setting. A good director who is trying to incorporate product placement into a scene might have a character pull a certain can of soda out of the refrigerator and continue a conversation while drinking the soda, but the director would not have a character pull a can of soda out and drink it in an unnatural setting, such as during a high speed car chase.

Product placement can be an effective means of advertising something without it seeming like a huge commercial. Consider the example of cigarettes; when the ban on using television commercials to advertise cigarettes went into effect in 1971, some cigarette companies instead turned to movies to get their products seen by potential customers. Tobacco companies paid a handsome fee to movie producers, and in return, film characters were seen smoking certain brands of cigarettes.

A good director has the ability to incorporate products into scenes while always keeping in mind the experience of the moviegoer. The trick is to keep the product in a natural setting, while also keeping the emphasis on the product as subtle as possible, but ensuring that viewers turn their attention to that product. It can be incredibly effective, even if the viewer's gaze on the product is for only a couple of seconds.

Low-profile wealthy

Not all people who is wealthy look as though they are. You already know not to assume that someone is not wealthy simply based on their appearance or demeanor, but in order to effectively market and sell to affluent people who keep a low profile, you need to understand a little more about them.

Why would someone choose to not flaunt his or her wealth? There can be many reasons. Perhaps the customer spent a large portion of his or her life not being wealthy, and as a result of his or her slowly built wealth, the customer retains some purchasing habits from before he or she had money. The customer might balk at buying an item at full price, even if he or she has more than enough money to spare for the purchase. Extravagance might make the customer uncomfortable, and he or she might feel uneasiness when referred to as affluent.

The question becomes how to compel people in this group to part with their money. For this group, you will obviously not try to aggressively push a sale or point out how shiny or flashy your product is. Instead, a better tactic might be to gently remind people from this group that they deserve to indulge occasionally or, if the product or service you offer is not a luxury item but instead is something generally regarded as necessary, point out how the item or service makes life easier or can make things run more smoothly. For example, suppose you lease the services of private jets, including pilots and attendants. Someone from the low-profile wealthy group might be reluctant to indulge in this expense when he or she can purchase a commercial ticket instead, so the key to selling the service in this situation is to emphasize the necessity, as well as the convenience. There is a right way and a wrong way to do this:

- **Wrong tactic:** "You deserve to be pampered when you travel, right? Why bother with the same traveling hassles that regular people have to endure?"

- **Right tactic:** "The ease and convenience of having access to a private jet for your personal and business travel will allow you to concentrate on what is really important in your life."

People who fall into the group of the low-profile wealthy might not want to be segregated from "regular people," as they might have fit into that group before acquiring their wealth. Think of it this way: Affluent people who choose not to live an extravagant lifestyle do so for a reason. They might be embarrassed by ostentatiousness, or they might have moral standpoints against excess. Aggressively presenting one of these customers with an item or service they do not need might result in a lost customer.

Many low-profile wealthy people do indulge in extravagance, but they do not necessarily flaunt their purchases. Going back to the example of the private jet, these customers might buy things that average consumers can only dream about, but they probably do not do so because they want to indulge or because they feel as though they deserve to live better than other people. They purchase access to private jets because it cuts hours off their total travel time and they will have more freedom when it comes to planning personal and business travel.

Remember that generalizations of affluent customers — and any other customers for that matter — do not apply to everyone. Some low-profile wealthy people might frequently make impulse buys of expensive items that are nothing more than indulgences, just as some high-profile wealthy people might cling to their money intently and only appear high profile because of the jewelry and vehicles companies allow them to borrow. The bottom line is that you can never know exactly how a customer will react to a product or service, even if you know the customer's upbringing, the amount of money in his or her bank account, and the history of his or her previous spending behavior. Human beings are somewhat predictable in their behavior, but there is no way to accurately predict spending behavior 100 percent of the time.

On the other hand, understanding the psychology behind the spending behavior of the wealthy can point you in the right direction when developing your marketing campaigns and selling tactics. Think of it as an interstate highway you can follow while always keeping in mind that there are many alternative routes, all of which can lead to the eventual destination: a sale.

Common traits of the wealthy

Matt Oechsli is considered an expert in the field of psychographic profiles of affluent-consumer spending behavior. Psychographics refer to the psychological reasoning behind the purchases consumers make. Instead of analyzing how consumers make purchases, the reasoning behind their purchases is analyzed. In his article "Psychografics: Profiling the Affluent Mind," Oechsli asserts that four factors are incredibly important to affluent customers. The following factors have a huge effect on whether an affluent customer is willing to part with his or her money:

1. Personal health

2. Family health

3. Financial health

4. Spiritual health

When all of these factors are balanced, affluent customers are much more likely to be comfortable with making major purchases. For example, an affluent customer who is facing a major health crisis might worry about the potential financial impact of that illness, whether it is the total cost of the necessary health care or the potential loss of profit from being unable to be as productive as before the illness. Likewise, if an affluent customer senses financial difficulties on the horizon, he or she is less likely to be able to convince the customer to spend money on unnecessary things. This is one trait that is relatively universal among most consumers; if the fear of economic problems is looming, most people find ways to eliminate unnecessary spending. Affluent customers can be affected by economic problems just as any other customers can.

Other common traits of wealthy people include tenacity and discipline. Many affluent people did not come from money and, therefore, had to work hard to get to where they are today. If a customer visits your business wearing a designer suit and a Rolex, you should not assume that he does not know a thing or two about a hard day's work. A person with a great deal of work ethic will naturally expect the same work ethic from the people with whom he or she does business. Suppose this customer wants something you sell that is out of stock. He or she will probably not accept "It is out of stock" as a final answer. Instead, the customer will assume that the next words out of your mouth should be "… but I will find a way to get it to you today."

About Your Customers

Affluent people generally believe in themselves and think big, which is something to consider when feeling apprehensive about attempting to sell an expensive item to an affluent person. If the customer wants the product, the customer will figure out a way to get it.

Many self-made affluent people also have a great deal of courage. It takes courage to come from nothing and build wealth because of the inevitable risks involved. Although most people avoid certain risks because there is too great a chance of failure, affluent people will go forward and give it their best efforts because they look toward the ultimate goal instead of to the potential obstacles.

Many affluent people are adept in social situations. This is one of the reasons they wind up being so successful; they can often make other people feel comfortable while also asserting their own opinions and ideas. They know how to work a room and can have powerful personalities. This is an important trait to know about your potential customers; they can be intimidating, but they will probably not respond well to a salesperson or representative who cannot hold his or her own. Affluent customers are used to people keeping up with them, responding to their demands, and being decisive. If you cannot present a confident and upbeat attitude when dealing with wealthy clients, you have a limited chance of being successful in marketing and selling to this target market. Shake your timidity and train your representatives to also soothe their nerves before dealing directly with affluent customers.

The affluent entrepreneur

Affluent entrepreneurs are a special breed of wealthy customers. Plenty of affluent customers can be aggressive, but entrepreneurs can be incredibly forceful and might even come off as rude, even if that is not their intent. They work hard, they juggle a wide variety of projects at once, and as far as they are concerned, they should not have to waste time when they want to buy something they know they want. Entrepreneurs might abruptly leave if they do not feel as though their needs are being met by a merchant or service provider, and furthermore, they will make sure everyone they know hears about their disappointment. And make no mistake about it, entrepreneurs have plenty of social connections.

They also are incredibly good at communication. When entrepreneurs tell you they want something, they will know exactly what they want and there will be little room for alternatives. If you cannot understand what an entrepreneur wants, he or she will probably get frustrated and maybe even a little upset. Listen carefully to what an entrepreneur tells you so you do not have to ask questions that have already been answered.

Do not be surprised if you find yourself drawn to affluent entrepreneurs on a business and personal level; a common attribute of this group is that they have infectious personalities and a type of magnetism that is difficult to describe. They can be just as charming as they can be assertive, which certainly makes for an interesting mix of personality traits to have as a customer. You might be hard pressed to convince this group they need something they do not want, and you will also have a difficult time retaining this group as customers if you do not deliver what they want promptly.

The affluent employee

Most people think of business owners or celebrities when they think of the affluent population, but there are many people who fall into the category of wealthy yet are employees of someone else. Which employees are pulling in salaries that qualify them as affluent? According to the Bureau of Labor Statistics, employees in the following positions earn over $100,000 annually and have the top highest-paying careers:

1. Surgeons

2. Anesthesiologists

3. Orthodontists and oral surgeons

4. Obstetricians and gynecologists

5. General internists

6. Physicians

7. Family and general practitioners

8. Chief executive officers

9. Psychiatrists

10. Pediatricians

11. Dentists

12. Podiatrists

13. Lawyers

14. Natural sciences managers

15. Prosthodontists

16. Engineering managers

17. Computer and information systems managers

18. Marketing managers

What trends do you notice when looking at the list? One of the obvious factors is that people who fall into these categories are educated. Successful surgeons and information system managers must have a high level of intelligence, or they will certainly not succeed in their chosen career fields.

Another common trait among these career fields is that these people are willing to work hard to get what they want. It is nearly impossible to become a psychiatrist without plenty of schooling and training, as well as competition.

Note that affluent people who are employees typically have a certain level of contentment with their positions. Why does a dentist stay an employee instead of opening a private practice? Why does a marketing manager stay with a company instead of becoming a consultant? Some people work as an employee because their college student loans are still being repaid, but many of them simply do not mind being an employee. An entrepreneur would shudder at the thought of working for someone else and relying on an employer for a paycheck, but affluent employees might eagerly embrace this position. They are willing to work hard and are compensated well for doing so.

When relying on a paycheck, affluent employees might be more careful with their money than someone who knows money will come in no matter what happens. For example, a lawyer who relies on his or her law firm for a salary knows that if the law firm folds or if he or she makes a major mistake and is fired, the money stops coming in. On the other hand, an affluent customer who is wealthy as a result of generational wealth might not have the same caution with spending because the money is not conditional.

Of course, affluent employees are a varied bunch. Some people in this group scramble to keep up with their neighbors with regards to the flashiest car, biggest house, and costliest landscaping design. The difference is that the reliance on an employer for a salary can make this type of lifestyle a tightrope act; lose the job and suddenly the employee can no longer afford the bonanza of expenses. On the other hand, plenty of affluent employees are careful with their finances and generally only buy things they need and can afford, so when the money abruptly stops coming in, they simply dip into their well-stocked bank accounts to survive until they can find another job.

How do you market to affluent employees? Cater to their needs and show them a great deal of respect. Remember that people in certain occupations not only spent several years learning what they know, but they also help people every day. For example, a salesperson should refer to her customer as "Dr. Smith," not as "Mr. Smith" or "Bob" because not acknowledging the proper title of the customer is an immediate insult.

Now that you have a good idea about the profiles of your potential wealthy customers, read on to learn about how to locate these customers.

CASE STUDY:
ADVICE FROM A
MARKETING EXPERT

Stephen Woessner
Marketing expert and author of
The Small Business Owner's Handbook
to Search Engine Optimization

The fundamental benefit of having an affluent customer base is you can charge more, without gouging, and you are less likely to be counted on for price. You can charge a healthy margin. Affluent customers are less likely to quibble about price. They are value buyers, not price sensitive shoppers.

The second thing is the audience is passionate and engaged, so once you are in the market, you will get more solid referrals. My mother ran a bakery and was not in the market for grocery store birthday cakes; her market was executives who were willing to pay $85 for their 2-year-old's birthday cake so they could say they bought their cake from Evie's Bakery. That is why the affluent market is so great; you will get powerful and engaged endorsements versus "I bought this at Walmart." Dealing with affluent customers has the potential to feed and grow itself if you stay engaged in the market. Both of these goals take time because it takes guts to charge more and stay consistent with your marketing strategy.

It is more expensive to open a store that caters exclusively to affluent people. It takes time to build your referral base. People take a shorter route and see their margins water down and then compete on price, which is a counterproductive strategy.

Chapter 2

The Search Begins

> *"The secret of success is to do the common things uncommonly well."*
>
> John D. Rockefeller, industrialist and philanthropist

R elying on customers to come to you might work in some situations, but when your goal is to target the affluent, you might find that you spend a great deal of your time hunting for new customers, making connections, and painstakingly building your reputation and brand before you ever see real results. Affluent customers are targeted by marketing tactics frequently simply because they have money to spend. After all, these customers have what marketing professionals call "disposable income," which means they have extra money to spend on luxury items after their essentials have been paid for. It makes sense that people constantly want to take them to lunch, meet with them at their places of work, or chat on the phone in an effort to convince them that they should buy the latest product or greatest service.

For this reason, do not be surprised if lukewarm marketing tactics do not yield results with the affluent crowd. Sending an unsolicited form letter that is not even personally signed or calling a potential customer from a crackly phone connection is just as bad as not trying to begin with. You need to go out and find these customers and make a connection with them if you have hopes of successfully marketing and selling to them. Only after you have built your customer base and created an appealing image for yourself can you hope to rely on word-of-mouth advertising to provide you with new customers. Until then, you need to determine how to locate customers who can make you successful.

How do you Locate Wealthy Customers?

You have already learned about the importance of understanding the backgrounds and spending habits of affluent people, but this information does not do you much good if you do not know how to locate wealthy customers in the first place.

Here is an important piece of advice: Marketing and selling to affluent customers is disproportionately comprised of building social relationships with them. Marketing campaigns can be great, but when dealing with this particular group of consumers, you will have to get to know them. What are their names? Where do they come from? When are their wedding anniversaries? What are their favorite types of wine? These are the questions you should be able to answer quickly about any affluent customer, and the only effective way to do this is to build genuine relationships. Take an interest in the things your customers say and ask questions. Treat an affluent customer as you would treat a friend who you greatly admire and respect. Remember that affluent customers are constantly barraged by people who care about nothing more than compelling them to part ways with their money. If you can offer a genuine relationship with customers, this will certainly set you apart from the other businesses trying to get their attention.

If you are the type of person who has no trouble forming relationships with people, you might not even stop to wonder how you should go about getting to know your customers. It is likely that you already have a knack for having natural conversations that lead to learning more about people while also making them feel at ease with the situation. Not everyone has this innate ability, however, so for some people the idea of forming personal relationships with potential and existing customers is a relatively terrifying proposition.

You do not have to take on a new personality when getting to know affluent people, but it helps if you defer to learning more about them instead of talking about yourself. Of course, do not try to shroud yourself in mystery, but instead of going on and on about your college years or your children, ask people about their college years, their children, and any other interesting topics that get people talking. The key to forming a relationship with your potential or existing affluent customers is to find out more about them and genuinely be interested in the things they have to say. Not only does this give you more information that might come in handy in the future, but people who are highly accomplished usually have interesting tales to tell. In the course of regaling you with interesting stories, affluent people will feel more comfortable with you and perhaps even begin to trust you. Instill a sense of trust into your affluent customers, and there is an excellent chance you will be the first person they think of when they want to purchase a product or service you provide.

This is not to say you should expect to become best friends or force a relationship on a customer who does not want a personal association with you. Instead, you need to go the extra mile to get to know your customers in order for them to trust you. Your knowledge will also help you to sense when it is appropriate to suggest another purchase or upgrade services.

So how do you find wealthy customers so you can start forming these relationships? You need to know where to find customers and how to recognize them. *You will learn more about locating afflu-*

ent customers later in this chapter and in subsequent chapters. *If*
have hopes of becoming successful in selling to the affluent, you
need to be proactive and bring the customers to your business
instead of waiting for them to come to you. Once you have these
customers, you need to pay particular attention to the things they
talk about.

About Your Customers

Keep a file on all your frequent customers. The file
should list birthdays, anniversaries, and special interests (for example, golf or theater) — not just a
history of their business transactions. Review this file periodically,
especially before meeting with your customer.

The places

You will most likely not encounter affluent people wandering the
aisles of a large discount store in the middle of the night. Go to the
places where affluent people go. Join racquetball and golf clubs
in affluent neighborhoods. Volunteer to serve on the board of a
philanthropic organization. If you attend church, attend church
in an affluent area. The point is to insert yourself into the affluent
culture by going to the places wealthy people go. Not only will
you have the opportunity to witness the behavior and habits of
affluent people firsthand, which should give you a leg up on the
competition who has not taken the time to do so, but you can also

form social relationships with the people who might eventually become your customers.

Simply put, the affluent social circle can be quite tight. Wealthy customers might be more likely to buy from you if they have already seen your face before or if you know someone they know. You have to go where the wealthy people go if you hope to make your face recognizable to the people to whom you are trying to offer a product or service. Go where affluent people go, and do what affluent people do to increase your chances of being accepted into this subculture with the ultimate goal of gaining trust from these potential customers.

The look

Some people send out an aura of affluence that is unmistakable. Whether it is the designer clothing or the way they walk into a room and immediately commands attention and respect, it can be easy to tell these people are wealthy — or at least that they are attempting to portray the image of an affluent person.

Unfortunately for you, however, potential customers do not walk around with their credit lines written across their foreheads or carry a sign featuring the amount of money in their deposit accounts. A well-dressed person might not be able to pay rent because of his or her shopping habits, and a person who commands a room might be charismatic and know human behavior as the result of having worked in a restaurant for years. So while first glances at potential customers might reveal affluence, do not rely solely on this initial encounter to decide that a person is wealthy. Take appearance with a grain of salt, but do not discount your initial impression right away. As you get to know the affluent, you will undoubtedly develop a sixth sense about who is affluent and who is merely playing the part.

Can physical attractiveness actually predict wealth? A number of studies have been conducted on this topic, and the results are mixed. One study conducted by Irene Hanson Frieze and her colleagues published in the *Journal of Applied Social Psychology* found that attractiveness can lead to higher starting salaries for males and higher eventual salaries for females, but with "attractiveness" being such a subjective trait, it is difficult to account for all the various factors that can come into play when studying anything related to physical attractiveness. Does this mean every attractive person you encounter is probably affluent? No, but it does mean that there is an increased chance that an attractive person makes more money than an average-looking counterpart. One thing to consider is that people who are physically attractive might simply present themselves in a more confident manner, and because confidence is a common trait among the affluent, there might be a correlation in some way between confidence, attractiveness, and affluence.

On the other hand, many of the most successful salespeople are those who simply assume that every customer has the financial ability to buy a product. Instead of assuming a customer cannot afford an expensive item because the customer is too young, too old, too plain, or too quiet, these salespeople treat every customer with the same respect and urgency. The truth is that not all customers allow their appearances to reveal their income level, and some customers who are not wealthy will find a way to make the purchase if their hearts are set on the item. Do not fall into a pattern of profiling potential customers with cursory glances and disregarding anyone who does not appear to be wealthy by the standards you expect to encounter. When you are in the beginning stages of building up a solid customer base, assume everyone who expresses interest in your product or service can afford what you offer.

 ## About Your Customers

Physiognomy studies the association between facial characteristics and behavioral tendencies. One study found that people with attractive facial features are more likely to have higher annual incomes while another study found that people with attractive facial features are more likely to be deemed as trustworthy. This does not mean that all your wealthy customers will be attractive, but it might be a good reason to try whenever possible to employ representatives who are attractive.

When the physical appearances of customers do not reveal enough information to help you ascertain their affluence or lack

thereof, rely on other clues. The wealthy can often shov
fluence by the things they do and the places they visit.

The habits

Affluent people often are comfortable in social situations. There
is something about accomplishing wealth that makes a room full
of people seem less intimidating, and this can be seen when affluent people walk through a room. Do they stop to chat with several people? Do people seem to want to pull them aside to talk?
Although it is true that there are affluent people who are socially
awkward, the majority of people who reach affluent status do so
in part because of their ability to network and relate to a wide
range of people. People who lead companies and who employ
large numbers of people have to compel people to trust them,
and it takes a socially adept person to pull that off.

Affluent people might also scan a room and notice the details
around them. Affluent people are often quite detail oriented, and
as a result, there is not a lot that escapes their attention. Look for
the person who appears to be in control and does not seem to be
lost in thought or highly distracted. If you are in a setting where
money is being spent, pay close attention to the purchases being
made. A person in a restaurant who pays the tab for a table full
of people who are there to socialize and not talk business is probably someone who can afford to do so, particularly if he or she
pulls out a platinum credit card.

Here is an important caution: Not everyone who is flashy with money is wealthy, just as not everyone who acts frugal is broke. Although the previous information can be used as a guideline, always keep in mind that there is no cookie-cutter method for spotting the habits of affluent people. In a recent study "Signaling Status with Luxury Goods: The Role of Brand Prominence," published in the *Journal of Marketing*, the authors point out that there are two different types of luxury: loud and quiet. Some customers prefer luxury simply for the sake of luxury and do not necessarily care if other people notice (quiet luxury) while other customers want to make sure their luxuries are noticed by other people (loud luxury). Instead of always looking for loud luxury, keep an eye out for quiet luxury, as well, and you will have a better chance of spotting potential customers.

In other words, just because a person does not display outward signs of wealth, it does not mean he or she is not indeed wealthy. Affluent people who prefer quiet luxury will have clothes that are well made and will drive cars that are luxurious, but you might not immediately recognize the clothes as being from a particular designer or might not spot these customers driving cars that are overtly affiliated with luxury. How can you tell if a customer can actually afford the expensive items you offer? Again, the best tactic is to just assume all of your customers have the means to buy whatever it is you are selling. Simply put, not every wealthy person exudes an air of affluence, and you do not want to miss these customers by not giving them the attention and service they deserve.

CASE STUDY:
PERSONALIZE
THE RELATIONSHIP

Matthew T. Seevers, Ph.D.
Assistant professor of marketing
Creighton University

There are a number of effective approaches that do not hinge on a consumer's income level. One approach is to offer a high level of value regardless of the price point. In other words, if a consumer anticipates receiving an excellent product relative to the asking price, this is likely to be successful whether the product is priced high or low. Another approach is to build trust with the consumer. For example, if a consumer comes to believe a seller is looking out for his or her best interests, he or she is more likely to not only repurchase from the seller but also to tout the seller to others. A third approach that is likely to be universally effective is to genuinely personalize the relationship. Many customers like to feel they are understood as individuals. And though this technique is perhaps more commonly applied in luxury settings, I believe it holds across most consumers.

The people

In general, most people like to socialize with other people who are of a similar socioeconomic status. Although this is not always the case, it is generally the norm, so assume people who are wealthy are generally going to socialize with other wealthy people.

Wealthy people are typically plugged in to their communities, so they will have friends and acquaintances who are well-known, such as politicians and other local celebrities. Even if affluent people are introverted, there is an excellent chance that people within the community at least know of them. Look for affluent people around other leaders, such as in community organizations or other groups. The people who step up to lead charitable organizations and other community projects are often people who are leaders in other areas of their lives, too. Because you already know that leadership and tenacity are common traits among affluent people, look to these people when trying to seek out affluent customers.

About Your Customers

A study appearing in *International Social Science Review* suggests that affluent people tend to socialize largely with other wealthy people as a way to affirm their own elite status. The same study also suggests that affluent people seek out social situations with other affluent people, such as in golf or tennis clubs, because they assume they will not be exposed to people from other socioeconomic groups who might not behave in the same way they do.

Genuine relationships

Note that you are not trying to trick people into liking you or to form fake relationships in order to gain the trust of your potential customers. Instead, think of the relationship building as one of the single most effective marketing tactics you can hope to use. However, it is only as effective as you are genuine. Many affluent people have grown so accustomed to being approached by people that they can spot a fake right away. You should want to get to know your customers, and you should want to frequent the same places your prospective future clients visit. If you have no desire to do so, you either need to aggressively pursue other marketing tactics or find a different demographic to target in your marketing efforts.

Allowing yourself to socialize with affluent people will give you the confidence you need to sell to them. Wealthy people can be quite intimidating, but by watching them in their everyday interactions, you will soon realize they are not quite as intimidating as you might have initially thought. Think of this along the lines of jumping out of airplane for your first skydiving experience; at first, the experience is terrifying, but once you experience it, jumping out of an airplane becomes something you enjoy as opposed to something that is fodder for nightmares. If you are intimidated by your customers, there is a good chance you will miss some great opportunities to market your products or services.

The patterns

As with most other consumers, you can count on affluent customers to stick with the things they like and adjust their spending when the economy performs poorly. You can also expect affluent customers to seek out luxury, even if it is something as simple as softer bed sheets or as indulgent as a luxury hotel suite. Affluent customers generally are not willing to be inconvenienced in order to save money, such as shopping at a retailer with horrible customer service with the intent of saving a dollar or two.

A common pattern among most affluent people is the habit of pampering themselves once in a while by getting massages or booking an exotic vacation for some rest and relaxation. Most affluent people understand the importance of occasional pampering, though there are certainly plenty of wealthy people who see pampering as a daily necessity. The point is that you can expect affluent people to be receptive to buying goods and services that serve as a way to help them feel rejuvenated or relaxed. It can be interesting to observe that the people in a crowded room who appear to be the healthiest and well kept are frequently the affluent people within the group simply because they can afford to buy the products and services available to help them stay healthy. They can afford the yoga retreats and the organic food, though this does not by any means guarantee that all affluent people take advantage of these options. Plenty of affluent people indulge in fast food and shirk exercise.

Affluent people will probably not appear intimidated when walking into an expensive boutique or showroom. Do not be surprised if the affluent are drawn toward sales, however, because this is a universal pattern among all consumers. Simply put, most consumers — affluent people included — do not want to feel as though they are missing out on a deal by paying full price for something. For this reason, do not label a customer as not being affluent simply because his or her first stop is at the sale rack or he or she has a coupon in hand. If all other signs point toward affluence, he or she is probably a wealthy customer who happens to love a good deal.

In particular, affluent customers are increasingly looking to the Internet to conduct research on products, as well as to find the lowest prices for the products they do buy. Do not assume that a customer who can afford to pay full price will do so willingly. The book *The Art of Selling to the Affluent: How to Attract, Service, and Retain Wealthy Customers & Clients for Life*, a 2004 study from the Oechsli Institute, suggests that affluent customers are acutely aware of the cost of the items they consider buying.

How do you Target Wealthy Customers?

You can profile affluent customers all you want, but unless you know how to target them and get them interested in whatever you are offering, you might wind up with nothing more than an acute talent for figuring out when a wealthy person enters the room. Although this might make for an interesting way to pass the time while waiting in line at the bank or waiting for a friend to arrive at a restaurant, being able to spot wealthy people is not going to make you money. On the other hand, if you use your talent for spotting affluent customers as an important step in a multistep process, you are setting yourself up to succeed.

About Your Customers

Do not disregard your own appearance when dealing with affluent customers. Ensure your salespeople are neatly groomed and wear clothing conducive to the environment. Just as it would be ridiculous to expect workers doing manual labor to show up in three-piece suits, it is equally absurd to allow salespeople representing expensive products to show up in tattered and stained clothing.

The balanced life

As previously mentioned, wealthy customers prefer to live balanced lives before they are willing to part with their money on unnecessary expenses. This balance is important, and if you attempt to unbalance things when selling or marketing to an affluent person, you might get a negative reaction.

Consider this scenario. Suppose you recognize that a man at a social gathering is affluent and you attempt to strike up a conversation. Because of your self-confidence and lively conversation, he is open to chat with you for a little while, and the conversation goes well — despite the fact this his young children frequently interrupt with requests for one thing or another. You are feeling pretty good about the connection you have established, and you discover that he is a fan of theater, so you jump right into a sales pitch about a stage production you are seeking investors for. You suggest that he jump on board before the chance is gone. Because you believe in the production — and any good salesperson should absolutely believe in the product or service he or she sells — you feel there is no way that someone who appreciates the arts would say no to investing money he or she can probably afford to lose anyhow.

The biggest problem with this sales pitch is that it was incongruous to the setting. The affluent man is trying to enjoy a social situation and spend time with his family, as is evident by the interruptions from his children. He cannot listen intently to your sales pitch because it is imbalanced with his goal of having a fun time. The conversation would have made much more sense if it had been initiated when the man was not spending time with his family but instead was in a business mindset.

How should this situation have been approached? Approaching the affluent customer for conversation was a great start, and working the topic of theater into the conversation was an excellent step. The clues that he was trying to have social time instead of work time should have been picked up on, and the theater subject should have been further explored. Business cards should have been exchanged, a follow-up phone call or e-mail inviting him out for lunch or coffee should have been sent out the following business day, and in the resulting meeting, the topic of the production needing investors would have been appropriate to insert into the conversation. You must decide whether to mention the investment opportunity when contacting the person to set up the lunch meeting; there are pros and cons to each approach. If you tell the person beforehand, he might decide not to meet with you. On the other hand, if you wait to tell the person until the two of you have met, you run the risk of making him feel as though he was tricked into the meeting. Use your best judgment based on the rapport you have already built with the potential investor.

About Your Customers

If you take a prospective client to dinner or coffee, pick up the tab. It would be incredibly rude to invite a prospective client out and then expect him or her to pay the bill, regardless of how much money he or she has. It is not a matter of who has more money; it is a matter of business etiquette. Remember to save the receipt and log it as a business expense for a possible deduction at tax time.

This tactic is not suitable for all situations, and the method by which you contact existing customers will be different from how you initially court a potential customer with whom you have never done business. When targeting potential customers, you need to maintain a delicate balance of aggressiveness and patience. Infuse the topic of what you do for a living into the conversation in a natural way, and you might find that the other person expresses interest before you even get to present a sales pitch. Mentioning that you own a jewelry boutique and handing over a business card at the end of the conversation might be all you need to do to see your new acquaintance at your boutique the next day, ready to browse, and more importantly, ready to spend. The trick is to keep your conversations balanced so that the potential customer stays comfortable. It is acceptable to assault a stranger with information about your jewelry boutique when you meet the stranger at a jewelry convention, but not when you meet at a party.

The affluent as consumers of services

People who grew up without wealth probably formed ideas from a young age about what they would do if they grew up to be rich. Some dreamed that they would never clean their own house or that they would hire educated nannies to help raise their children. If these people grow up and find themselves affluent, they are in the enviable position of actually being able to make these dreams come true.

Target this market by letting them know how easier their lives will be with the service you provide while also reminding them that they deserve to have someone else handle the tedious chores. Take care to word the pitch carefully. "Please allow us to manage your home while you attend to the truly important things in life," sounds much better and more appealing than "Hire us to clean your house." Also, keep in mind that if you attain one customer in an affluent neighborhood, treat that customer like gold because this might serve as your gateway to other nearby homes. People within affluent neighborhoods often wind up privileged because of their competitive drive, so when Mr. Johnson sees that Mr. Smith hires a new company to mow his lawn, Mr. Johnson might decide that he should also hire the same company to do his lawn and his landscaping. If it is your truck in Mr. Smith's driveway and your van prominently features your telephone number, you just might wind up with a phone call from Mr. Johnson. Treat every job and every encounter as a potential moment to gain more customers.

Depending on the type of rapport you have with your customers, you might be able to network directly through some of your customers. There is nothing wrong with approaching one of your affluent customers and mentioning that a client referral will result in a free service for him or her. For example, if you clean houses and your current client refers a friend to you who then signs a contract with your company, you could offer the first client one free housecleaning. This shows your customers you appreciate the referral and helps you gain more business.

Always carry business cards with you while providing a service to someone in an affluent neighborhood. Suppose you provide errand-running services to a customer who lives in an expensive high-rise condo. You are standing in the elevator with dry cleaning and packages and another resident steps onto the elevator and strikes up a conversation. You have a few floors to let that person know about the services you provide, and unless you have a business card, there is a good chance your opportunity to get a new client will leave when the resident steps off the elevator. Another good example would be a nanny who frequently takes the children in her care to the park to play. If she is approached by another mom who wants to know about the services she provides, a professional business card will make a much better impression than a name and phone number scribbled on the back of a used piece of paper.

Target these customers by offering convenience. A good dog groomer can get affluent customers, but a good dog groomer who does house calls will be highly sought after. Make your customers believe you will do everything to make them happy. For example, if you run a massage therapy business and one of your existing clients mentions his wife is pregnant and might like to have a massage, do not just nod and agree that it would be a good idea. Instead, offer to take your portable table to their home and schedule an appointment before he leaves. You might suggest that the massage should be a surprise for his wife, and if he would like, you would be willing to bring along flowers or a piece of jewelry that the client gives you to present to his wife to complete the experience. You might also bring along a small baby gift. If this sounds like too much work, think about the impression you are making. You are setting yourself apart from other service providers in a variety of ways, including:

- Your original client is impressed and appreciative of all your extra effort.

- The client's wife is amazed at all of the thought you put into the moment and becomes a regular client.

- Both the client and his wife tell the story to their affluent friends, perhaps even handing out the business cards you left with them.

Suppose the client's wife happens to have several other friends who also are pregnant. After the babies are born, you can offer to present a free workshop on infant massage to them. At the event, you can provide small gift bags of baby toys, relaxing candles or lotions for the moms, and of course, additional business cards. You will spend less money on these little trinkets for your gift bags than you would on a comprehensive ad campaign, and you will make a much bigger impression.

After you locate affluent customers

After you are in contact with affluent customers, make sure you stay in contact with them. Send birthday greetings and handwritten cards to say hello. Call affluent customers when a product becomes available that you know they would appreciate and be interested in seeing. You simply cannot rely on one contact with an affluent customer to cement your relationship. You need to actively work toward staying in contact with these customers. The goal is to become the go-to person for whatever product or service you offer in the minds of your affluent customers.

Having a social relationship with your customers and maintaining contact with them will do you no good if you are not excellent at what you do. If you do not provide a high-quality product, or if the services you provide are not the best around, you will not hold on to your affluent customers for long, even if you send cards and make phone calls. Affluent customers already expect the things they buy and the services they pay for will be top quality, so if you are losing customers despite all of your best efforts to maintain contact with your customers, you might have to take a step back and examine what you are offering. Put a lot of effort into your marketing strategies, but do not concentrate so much on marketing that your product or service dwindles in quality.

Never think of affluent customers as one-time customers. People who have a great deal of wealth have the ability to make purchases repeatedly, even if the items they purchase are expensive and luxurious. Consumers who are not affluent might only ever purchase one designer bag because they just want to be able to say they own the bag. On the other hand, affluent customers might buy one designer bag, decide that they are fans of this particular bag, and then buy the bag in every color while also coming back every time a new bag design becomes available. Instead of regarding your affluent customers as one-time conquests, consider them as potential profit providers for years to come.

What do the wealthy expect?

Wealthy people expect to experience impeccable customer service. If they are going to shell out hundreds, thousands, or millions of dollars for the items and services they buy, they expect that they will be treated respectfully by everyone they encoun-

hroughout the entire transaction. That means the person who greets them at the front door, the representative who assists them, and the person who carries their purchases to the car should offer impeccable service. You cannot expect to retain affluent customers if the person who answers your business's phone is rude, no matter how wonderful and attentive the rest of your staff might be. For this reason, you need to make sure your employees exhibit the same respect and quality of service *you* offer. *Chapters 5 and 9 further discuss employees and customer.*

Some wealthy people — particularly high-profile wealthy people — expect that they will be known when they enter into a place of business. This means they will be addressed properly and treated respectfully. They should not have to ask for assistance because the assistance should be provided proactively. If a wealthy person returns for another visit, the person assisting him or her should remember the previous transaction and anticipate the customer's needs. This is why keeping meticulous files of everything about a customer, from birthdays to interests, is important.

Does this sound like a lot of work? It certainly can be in the beginning, but after you build relationships with your customers, it will become much easier. You will know what the customer wants, perhaps even before the customer knows what he or she wants.

Affluent customers also expect to receive accurate information. Do not attempt to disguise your product return policy in the hopes of tricking an affluent customer into making an expensive purchase that cannot be returned. Do not promise to provide a service at a certain day and time and then show up two hours late when you knew all along that you would be unable to make the scheduled time. Do not make up answers that might not be true; if an affluent customer wants to know what the rate of return will be on an investment product, yet there is no data available to even estimate what it will be, tell the truth but frame it positively. Instead of saying, "I have no idea what the rate of return might wind up being," try telling the customer, "The rate of return could potentially be phenomenal, but without any accurate data available, I am not at liberty to speculate as to what your rate of return will actually be." These two statements basically say the same thing and tell the truth about the information, but only one of them mentions the possibility of an impressive return. The other statement does not provide enough information, and vague answers generally do not go over well with affluent customers. It boils down to this: Tell your customers the truth, even if you know they might not be happy about it. Phrase the truth in the best possible light, but do not avoid the truth. A customer who is lied to — affluent or not — is unlikely to become a repeat customer.

Give affluent customers what they expect. Provide the best service possible and provide a product or service that will be so impressive that your customers cannot help but spread the word about what you offer.

Remember, if you are at a loss for what your affluent customer wants, just ask. Although you should eventually be able to anticipate the needs and wants of your customers, you are not expected to read people's minds. Do not be afraid to clarify what your customer is looking for. It is far better to ask questions and get the answers you need to find out what your customer wants than it is to make an assumption based on no reliable information and consequently miss the mark substantially. Absolutely nothing is wrong with asking the simple question, "How can I help you today?" Most customers would much rather be asked to clarify their wants than to have someone make faulty assumptions.

CASE STUDY: ADVICE FROM A MARKETING EXPERT

Jeanne Grunert
Direct and online marketing expert
Seven Oaks Consulting

Marketing to affluent customers is different from marketing to other demographics. Affluent customers spend more money per transaction and expect service commensurate with their spending habits; the more they spend, the better service they demand. What passes muster as good customer service for other demographics might not satisfy the affluent.

Wealthy customers prefer to shop at exclusive stores and spend their money on status-symbol products. They crave limited-edition, imported, exclusive, and one-of-a-kind items; white-glove service; and extra attention, and they will pay for it. Affluent customers expect to be treated as unique individuals, and marketing programs such as a direct marketing program that customizes marketing pieces to the individual by name or interest often appeal more to the affluent demographic. Lastly, affluent customers often exert more influence over their peers than those in other demographics. Word gets around quickly about exceptional situations, both good and bad, so be sure your company is willing to handle each transaction with finesse and attention to detail.

Chapter 3

The Value
of Research

> *"If one does not know to which port one is sailing, no wind is favorable."*
>
> Seneca, ancient Roman philosopher

When you make the decision to market and sell to an affluent customer base, you are deciding to target a select group of consumers who have the expendable financial resources that allow them to make purchases other groups cannot afford. However, you also are deciding to target a group of consumers who can, at times, be highly inaccessible. Affluent customers are frequently courted by people selling things, and for this reason, wealthy customers might learn how to disregard most attempts to get them to part with their money. Constant attempts from salespeople to get affluent people to make purchases can make them cynical to most of these attempts.

How can you actually catch the attention of affluent customers, even if they have grown accustomed to ignoring and disregarding the frequent marketing and selling attempts they encounter? One big step that should be taken before you start offering your product or service is to make sure there is actually a market for what you plan to offer. Do the affluent customers you plan on targeting actually have a need or want for what you plan to sell?

Market Analysis

The range of research you have to do in order to effectively offer goods or services to an affluent customer base can vary widely depending on several factors. The research you do before offering homemade gourmet dog treats will be different from the research you will do before opening a large, upscale shopping center in the heart of an affluent area. Regardless of the product or service you offer, it is important to analyze your potential customer base before assuming your target customers will welcome your offerings with open arms.

Simply put, the point is to find out whether there is actually a need or want for whatever you want to offer. Occasionally, it will be obvious that there is already a need for the service or product you want to provide. For example, suppose you enjoy making homemade fudge and frequently bring batches into your place of work. All of your coworkers rave about the fudge, and it does not take long before the people around you start asking to buy batches. You then receive an e-mail from one of the executives in the company who tried a piece of the fudge in the office break room and loved it. The executive wants to purchase a large batch of fudge for an upcoming executive retreat. This parlays into all of the executives at your place of work trying your homemade fudge, and before you know it, you have more orders than you can handle because word-of-mouth marketing about your home-made fudge has made your reputation explode. Orders for the fudge begin coming in from people you do not even work with. You increase the price of your homemade fudge, but people are still willing to buy it, and pretty soon, you find yourself thinking about quitting your day job to make fudge full time.

In this instance, it is obvious there is a desire for the product and that people are willing to pay a higher price for the product. Because the main audience responding to the homemade fudge is the group of executives within the company, it is feasible to market the fudge as a high-end product. It is also encouraging to note that the fudge is so well liked that word-of-mouth market-ing has propelled the fudge to social circles that extend beyond your own. The fact that the fudge became so popular without any marketing efforts on your part at all — with the exception of bringing in batches for people to nibble on at work — is another sign that this might be a successful business venture aimed at an affluent audience. Wealthy customers will be willing to spend more on fudge if it is the best fudge around, particularly if the people around them are talking about how great the fudge is.

Not all business ideas arise so accidentally and smoothly. Sometimes an idea for a product or service starts in the beginning stages without any real knowledge of whether wealthy people will respond well to the product or service. Consider a person who decides to open a gourmet coffee shop in an affluent area. She chooses an area that has a high concentration of wealthy people and takes steps to try to make the coffee shop appear as high-end as possible. Her coffee drinks and pastries are expensive and high quality. She makes sure the location of the coffee shop is near the local elementary school, which would allow parents the opportunity to use the drive-up window after dropping the children off at school. She assumes these factors alone will guarantee her business' success with the affluent customers living and working in the area.

The problem with her plan is that she did not do enough research. In this scenario, a large portion of the affluent population within the geographic area abstains from coffee as a result of their religious beliefs. So although she had the right idea to use a prime location conducive to a population that generally buys gourmet coffee drinks, the coffee shop owner did not take into consideration that the product she was offering was simply not something people in this particular area would want. Had she offered fruit smoothies or some other drink that is not frowned upon by the majority of the residents in the area, her business might have been a hit. If she had taken the time to get to know the population of the town she hoped to open a business in, it would have quickly become apparent that her idea of a coffee shop was not going to work for the affluent customer base she hoped to attract.

The Small Business Administration

An incredible amount of market analysis and market research information is available free of charge on the website for the Small Business Administration (**www.sba.gov**). Information available through the SBA includes statistics regarding income, religious affiliation, and employment for specific locations, among other things. This type of information will prove to be incredibly valuable when marketing to a specific area. Using the information provided by the SBA will help you realize if the customers in your area can actually financially support a business like yours; you would not want to start a brick-and-mortar specialty boutique for exotic (and expensive) perfumes if your city does not have a population wealthy enough to buy these products.

Even if you already have been in business for many years or even if your business does not necessarily fall under the category of "small business," periodically reviewing demographic information about the customers you hope to reach is a good idea. Demographics can change frequently, so assuming the population within a given location will stay steady forever is unwise.

Ask the important questions

Plenty of valuable research has already been done for you and can be found online beyond the SBA. Websites such as City Data (**www.city-data.com**) tell you important information to know before deciding to do business in a certain area, such as:

- **Income demographics:** Is there actually an affluent customer base in the area?

- **Home value estimates:** Is a downward trend of decreasing home values among all homes — including expensive homes — occurring in the area, which would point to an overall economic decline?

- **Existing businesses:** Is someone already offering what you want to offer?

- **Religious affiliations:** Are there predominant religious beliefs or restrictions within the area that will affect your potential for successful sales?

If there has not already been an interest in the product or service you intend to offer, make a point of talking to people in the community to find out the feasibility of starting a business that will provide certain goods or services. For example, if you hope to open a salon and day spa that caters exclusively to clients willing to pay a lot of money to receive the premier services available, visit the salons in the area and ask the owners about requested services these salons cannot cater to. You might find that salon owners in your area frequently get asked for reflexology or aromatherapy yet do not have the resources to offer these services. This gives you incredibly important information; potential competitors are not providing a desired service. Your exclusive salon can bridge that gap.

What if you cannot get the local business owners to confide in you about what customers are asking for? This might be a problem you run into; after all, your new business is going to be in competition with the other businesses. If you cannot convince the local business owners to give you this valuable information, you have other options you can explore.

Go directly to the source

Your hope is to market to an affluent customer base, so who better to ask about what they want than the people themselves? If you already are associated with an affluent circle, talk to people within this circle about what they would be willing to pay for and at what price. You have a distinct advantage if you have affluent friends who are willing to speak frankly about their needs and wants.

You might still be able to speak to potential customers even if you do not have affluent people within your social circle. Although you do not want to bombard affluent people with a clipboard and survey questions, you can make an attempt to find out where affluent people gather and then discern whether it would be appropriate to approach them in this setting. Suppose a businesswoman is thinking of opening a business that matches experienced nannies with families in need of quality child care. It would be completely appropriate for this businesswoman to approach an organized mothers' group in an affluent neighborhood that meets monthly and ask to speak to the group about what its members look for in nannies. Not only does this provide valuable feedback from the specific demographic the businesswoman hopes to appeal to, but it also introduces the mothers to the businesswoman and forms a relationship. When this woman opens her business, the women from the mothers' group might be among the first of her clients.

Observe from afar

Go to the places where affluent people go. If you want to open a retail store or boutique, spend a day wandering around high-end boutiques and expensive department stores and pay attention to what people are buying. If people linger around particular merchandise, determine what motivates them to actually make a purchase. Is it the way the salesperson talks to them, the ambience of the store, or something else? Are people even making purchases? If you intend to sell a particular type of merchandise, pay close attention to how customers react to similar items. Is there interest in the item? Are people excited by the item? Do people walk right past the item without so much as a glance?

You do not have to be a clinical psychologist to observe and understand human behavior. You can tell when shoppers are excited about certain items or when items make no impact whatsoever.

Just make sure the people you observe are the type of people you hope to attract in your business. You would not head to Kmart to observe consumer behavior if your intention is to solely market and sell to the affluent because you will not get an accurate depiction of the consumer behavior you want to understand. It is important to keep in mind that affluent consumer behavior is generally different from the consumer behavior of other people. You cannot lump affluent spending into the same category as the spending of the general population.

Get help

Not everyone is comfortable with trying to speak to affluent people about possible business ideas, but if no research is done beforehand to find out whether there is a need or want for the product or service you plan to offer, you are entering into business blindly without any real idea of what your potential for success — or failure — can be. Although it is important to eventually get over the fear of approaching affluent people if you plan to market and sell to them, there are ways you can initially obtain a market analysis without having to do all the work yourself.

Consider hiring a marketing agency or consultant to handle the process of finding out what types of people are in the area and what products and services appeal to them. Although this service will cost money, it can be an expense that is well worth it if the analysis yields the information you need in order to open a successful business. Remember that knowing what products or services the affluent people in your area want is only half the battle; you also must determine how to offer it to these customers in a way that is appealing to them. Finding out what the appeal of your product or service is will only get you so far, but it certainly is an important initial step.

This does not mean you should not do research on your own. Take what the professional says into consideration and use it as a valuable starting point for the direction you should take, but unless you are prepared to enlist the assistance of professional market-research consultants on a continual basis, you will have to get used to researching on your own. Remember that market research is not a one-time deal. As your customers' needs change, and as you decide to introduce new products or services or perhaps even branch out with regards to the areas you present your offerings to, you need to "go back to the drawing board" to make sure your ideas are feasible. You also want to ensure you are current on the needs of your customers so that you can offer exactly what they are looking for. If you have an existing customer base, periodically poll some of your customers — formally or informally — to find out what other products or services they wish you would offer. As you get to know your customers better, however, you will probably learn to anticipate their needs. Until then, though, do not be afraid to ask.

Preparing for online offerings

Your research methods are going to be different if you hope to primarily offer your products or services online instead of through a brick-and-mortar store or office where people can visit. If your main goal is to offer your product or service online, the first thing to do is go online and find out who your competition will be and determine how they offer their services.

For example, an Internet search for rare first edition books yields a variety of results, but the websites that are at the top of the non-sponsored links all have a few things in common. First, they all have beautifully designed websites that are visually appealing and free from any spelling or grammatical errors. They also all emphasize the word "rare" prominently throughout the website, which is an attractive attribute for affluent people who want to have things no one else has. Most of the websites also feature photographs of the actual books they sell and list the prices for the most expensive books right on the main Web page. Although spending $20,000 on a signed first edition copy of F. Scott Fitzgerald's *The Beautiful and Damned* might seem like an absurd purchase to most people, affluent people with the money to spend and an interest in rare books will look at the $20,000 price tag and consider the purchase completely reasonable. The book is unique because it is signed by the author and rare because it is a first edition print from 1922.

If your hope is to sell first edition books to an affluent audience, have a closer look at the websites of the successful online booksellers and find out what features are offered. This will be your competition, after all, so if you want to compete, you will need to not only offer the same features but offer more than your competition. If your competition offers a feature online that allows potential customers to send a message to a book expert, offer live chat features with book experts. If your competition offers online content about the art of book collecting, provide more information than they do in order to convey a sense of authority and knowledge. Simply put, you need to one-up the competition — but in a way that will still appeal to affluent customers.

About Your Customers

Use online tools to find out what people are looking for online. Try websites such as NicheBOT **(www.nichebot.com),** which will tell you whether people are searching online for what you plan on selling, and if so, how many people are searching on a monthly basis.

You should also pay attention to other valuable cues. Do all of the websites offering rare books appear to have recently lowered all their prices? Can you find information online about a recent decline in the purchase of rare books? Even something as random as a forum posting about how an online rare bookstore might have to close its virtual doors from lack of sales can be quite telling. If you are about to delve into a market that is currently in decline, this is something you want to know beforehand so that you can decide whether you want to go forth with your plans, wait to launch your business, or switch gears and sell something else entirely.

Without a little effort beforehand, you might quickly discover you have jumped into a business that is not doing well overall, which is something that can be learned with a few clicks of a computer mouse. The information is simply too valuable to not bother conducting before starting your business online.

Should you allow a recent economic decline to stop you from starting your business, even if your plan is to target affluent customers? The answer depends largely on the product or service you plan to offer. Studies have shown that not all affluent people scale back on their spending during tough economic times, but they might scale back on purchases that are considered flashy because they do not want to appear as though they have no empathy for the people affected. So although it might be safe to start a business selling high-end air conditioning units for residential structures that can be purchased and customized online — because, after all, affluent people want comfort and they want it from the most prestigious source available, regardless of the economy — you might want to think twice before starting a new jewelry store designed with affluent customers in mind who want the most opulent jewels available. Affluent people will keep the temperature of their homes comfortable during a recession, but they might be less likely to purchase a huge diamond necklace when so many people are out of work and suffering.

Research economic forecasts online using websites such as Wells Fargo **(https://www.wellsfargo.com/com/research/economics)** or MarketWatch **(www.marketwatch.com/economy-politics/calendars/economic)**. Although no economic forecast can tell the future, it makes good business sense to have an idea of what experts are predicting for the upcoming economic climate. Prior to the beginnings of the 2007 foreclosure crisis, many economic experts were already predicting that economic turmoil was imminent. This type of information is important for any business owner to know.

Know Who Your Customers Are

Knowing who your affluent customers are is not a matter of being able to spot them walking down the street, though this certainly is a talent that will serve you well after your business is up and running. Knowing your customers when initially putting your business together instead involves understanding whom among the affluent to target. It is an incredibly broad statement to say that you intend to market and sell "to the affluent" without further clarifying whom among them will be your focus.

The term "affluent" refers to a certain financial status but does not further clarify gender, occupation, age, or other factors that help you determine how you should market and sell to your customers. You will probably use different marketing and sales tactics to sell an expensive sports car to a young, single affluent gentleman than you would when attempting to sell a luxury minivan to an affluent housewife in her 40s. Although both customers are considered affluent and both are buying vehicles, they have different motivations for their purchases and will expect to be treated in different ways by a salesperson.

Although your product might appeal to a wide variety of affluent people, such as if you sell cars at a luxury car dealership,
it is important to remember that there is not one homogeneous
type of affluent person. There are affluent people who are highly
educated, and there are affluent people without much education
at all. There are affluent men and affluent women, and affluent
people can be young or old. Affluent people might be single or
married, might have children or not, and might be healthy or
perpetually ill. When figuring out who your target market will
be for your goods or services, go beyond merely saying your target market is affluent people and look closer at the subcategories
present.

Figuring out who your actual target market will be can be a simple task if you offer something most people need. For example, if
you plan to open a high-end market offering organic foods and
highly personalized attention, your market will likely appeal to
affluent people, regardless of gender, age, or occupation because
everyone needs to eat. On the other hand, if you plan to provide
dog-walking services to affluent neighborhoods, you can assume
you will only receive business from those affluent people who
have dogs. When you offer something specialized, such as dog-
walking services, wigs, party planning for children's birthday
parties, or anything else that caters to a specific segment of the affluent population, you need to do research beforehand to determine whether the need exists for your goods or services within
that specific segment of the affluent population.

CASE STUDY:
A FRANK DISCUSSION WITH
AN AFFLUENT CUSTOMER

Don Eckles
CEO
Boundless Enterprises

Don Eckles and his wife founded Scooter's Coffeehouse in 1998. They started with one small drive-through and quickly expanded to more than 80 stores in seven states. Voted "Best Coffee" in multiple locations, this company is a good example of how one person took a simple concept and turned it into a lucrative enterprise. Don joined the ranks of the affluent through hard work and perseverance combined with quite a bit of business savvy.

It is one thing to read research and data involving marketing and selling to affluent customers, but it is another thing to actually sit down and have a conversation with an affluent customer in order to find out what drives him or her to make purchases. Don agreed to answer questions regarding his own spending habits versus what research says regarding affluent customer purchasing behavior.

Question: Research suggests affluent customers display brand loyalty after they find something they like. Do you have loyalty to the brands you like?

Don: I think I probably do have brand loyalty, but I have not really thought about it. Some folks consider it conservative and stodgy to stick to one brand, but I do not think so. For example, I am a big fan of Toyota because they run forever. If I find a restaurant I like, I go there over and over again.

Question: Experts say that after an affluent customer finds something he or she likes, he or she is very likely to tell people about the product or service. Do you frequently tell your friends and family about the products or services you like?

Don: I do not think I do, partly because I am one of those guys who figures no one cares what I like. In the case of a steak house, I find it is awkward because you almost cannot talk about it; most people do not feel comfortable dropping $150 on dinner. I usually just do not talk about purchases. I am probably not a good customer anyway because I do not spend a great deal of time shopping. Take these pants for example: I have had them for ten years. One exception is that I do tell people what I like to eat when it is not an expensive place. Take Culver's, for example; if people talk about ice cream I ask them, "Have you ever had Culver's?" Their frozen custard is one of my favorites, and I can talk about this with almost anyone because it is affordable.

Question: Research suggests that affluent customers like to have the newest, nicest, top-of-the-line products. Is this true with you?

Don: That is true, whether it is gadgets or other things. I like to buy things that jump out and grab me. It is fun when I go out to buy something cool. There are some things I could not care less about, such as cereal and cold medicine. If I go to the store for cold medicine, and I find myself with the store brand in one hand for $5 and the name brand in the other hand for $7, I am going to choose the cheaper store brand because I figure either one is going to give me the results I need. However, when it comes to things like cars and shirts, I do care about having the nicest things possible. For example, the shirts I wear are expensive, but I prefer them because I like them more than inexpensive shirts. The expensive shirts are more comfortable and just nicer.

Question: Affluent customers are generally supposed to expect a higher level of customer service than average customers, according to research. When you walk into a store, are you expecting a high level of customer service?

Don: Yes, although I am not sure if that is because I am an affluent customer or because we are in a customer-service business. We are all selling something. Take Culver's again as an example; sometimes the customer service is great and sometimes the server abruptly says through the window, "$3.97" and then slams the window shut. If you do not care enough to smile at someone and greet him or her, you are in the wrong business. If I do not get good enough customer service, I just do not go back to that place.

I understand how important customer service is in my own company. Three or four years ago we had a meeting with our managers, and I could tell something was not right. It seemed some of the managers were just biding their time until something better came along. So we said, "Some of you who are here today will not be here at our next meeting because we are taking a new approach. If you do not buy into what we are doing, you will have to go." The very next day we had a person come in and say they had to move on. The people we have now understand this concept and want to serve a quality cup of coffee quickly.

Question: What marketing or selling techniques do not work when people are trying to get you to buy something?

Don: Here is what does not work on me: Making stuff up. I do not like it when people use words such as "unsurpassed" because some people think it must be the absolute best, but it really means there are many products out there that are just as good. Some salespeople will make up things about their competitors instead of why I should buy their product. I do not want to hear about why I should not buy the other guy's product; I want to hear about why I should buy your product. Do not oversell and underdeliver.

I want to be treated with respect. I do not want someone giving me a line of baloney. I am here, so assume I want to buy something. Listen to me and understand what I want to buy instead of concentrating on making your commission. Help me make my purchase; do not put the hammer on me. There is an old saying that goes "Don't talk yourself out of a sale." I believe in life we all sell regardless of what we do, but some of us have not figured it out yet.

Question: Has there been a time when you made a large purchase on impulse, and what compelled you to make the purchase?

Don: There are probably a lot of them from earlier in life than later. I bought a boat a few years ago that just sits in my garage most of the time. I was in this boat showroom, and I do not even remember why I was there to begin with, and here is this pontoon boat. All of a sudden I am thinking, "This is great! We can grill out on the lake!" It was not a practical purchase because we have to struggle to get it out of the

garage once a year, but it was an impulse buy. The salesperson certa[...]
ly had some impact on my decision to make the purchase because he
said that they had to clear the boat out, so they were willing to sell it to
me for $23,000 versus $28,000. So not only did that tell me that I would
not pay full price, but it also told me that if I left and came back later the
boat might no longer be there for me to purchase.

When we built our home we made some decisions that were made
based on emotion, but we always stayed within our budget. We put an
elevator in our new house, and while some people might wonder why
you would put an elevator in a house, I think it is pretty cool. I try to take
all my emotional stuff and put it into a price range so that any things we
want that are nice to have must fit into a budget. I have always believed
you have what you have to spend, and you have to choose wisely because you cannot spend it twice.

Sticking with affluent customers

You have done the market research necessary to find out whether
the specific segment of the affluent population you want to target is actually willing to buy what you are selling, and you have
opened your doors — literally or virtually — but you find the
temptation to try to tap into the other segments of the general
population is hard to resist. You cannot shake the thought that
including some lower-end offerings in your products or services
might attract customers who are not necessarily affluent but who
might be willing to spend a little extra to buy what you are selling.

Be careful when considering this option. When you are in the
initial phases of trying to create a name and reputation for yourself among affluent customers, it is vital that you retain an air of
exclusivity. Although it is true many luxury brands have suc-

cessfully broadened their accessibility and appeal to less-than affluent customers while still retaining affluent customers, such as
Jimmy Choo and Cadillac, remember that these brands started
out as luxury brands initially marketed and sold to affluent customers. It was not until years down the road that these companies were able to broaden their customer base without harming
their reputation and allure.

Chapter 4

Marketing Mastery

> *"The sole purpose of marketing is to sell more to more people, more often, and at higher prices. There is no other reason to do it."*
>
> Sergio Zyman, "New Coke" executive and motivational speaker

I f you have formally studied marketing, you are probably already familiar with the "Four P's:" product, price, promotion, and placement. These four factors should always be examined before offering a product or service for sale. In short, you should only offer a product or service if people will actually buy it. You can make sure your product is incredibly well-known, but if no one wants it, it will simply not sell. Even some of the best marketing campaigns fail miserably because there simply is not a market for the product. It is not enough to think that glittery, expensive products will sell well in your area because there are so many affluent people within the population. You need to think beyond initial assumptions and use marketing research techniques to determine whether your products will sell.

There is More to Marketing than Getting the Word Out

Maybe you have a superb product or offer services that are truly amazing. Although you can rely on word of mouth to start you down the path to success, it takes a great marketing strategy to push you across the finish line. Simply put, a large portion of your target market will never know about your product unless you tell them about it.

You must strike a delicate balance when marketing solely to wealthy customers. If this is truly the target market you hope to attract and you are not concerned with other customers, you might want to think twice before allowing word of your product or service to saturate all markets. Your product or service should have an air of exclusivity to it and should appear to only be available to the most prestigious clients and only in limited quantities. Affluent people are drawn to things that are not common. They want to own the things that no one else owns. For example, if you have three identical necklaces, only place one in your display case. If you sell luxury vehicles, do not litter the display area with a wide selection of cars. If you sell memberships to a country club, make sure everyone knows it can be difficult to be accepted into the club. If your marketing efforts can project the image that everyone cannot have what you have, you create a demand that appeals to affluent people.

Remember, creating demand will not work if your product or service is not worthy of the hype. Using the previous example of the country club, no matter how exclusive you make membership into the club, if the club does not have the amenities affluent people are looking for, they will not obtain the membership.

Consider the example of the American Express Centurion Card. This so-called "Black Card" was once spoken about in hushed tones and is still relatively veiled in secrecy. People know that the credit card exists and that it is only available by invitation directly from American Express. Other details of the card are not quite as well-known, such as how to actually get an invitation and what credit limits are on this card. Whether intentionally or unintentionally, American Express created a desire for a product among affluent people without investing in any overt advertising. You will not see commercials for this credit card on television, and you will not receive an invitation to apply for this card unless you are among the highly affluent. A person who pulls a Centurion Card out of his or her wallet is making a bold statement: "I am wealthy; I was sought out by American Express to accept a Centurion Card, and I have a credit card in my wallet that many people want but very few can actually get." American Express did not have to sell the idea of this card being desirable to the masses; the masses assumed the card was desirable because they could not get their hands on it.

You need to decide if your marketing strategy should involve saturating your target market with reminders of your product or if it would indeed be better to create a desire for your product by making it appear elusive and exclusive. It can be difficult when attempting to approach your marketing from both angles. How can you make your product appear incredibly exclusive while also making sure everyone knows about it? Depending on your product or service, this might be impossible. If you offer the exact same product a boutique across town offers, you are not going to have much luck trying to make your product appear elusive and exclusive. Then again, if you offer a product that is unlike any other products available because it is bigger, better, or unique in some other way, capitalize upon the things that make the product the best option for people who can afford to buy it.

Affluent people are generally quite savvy. A restaurateur who thinks she can slap together some beef patties and make the claim that she offers something special because she charges more for her hamburgers will quickly find out the customers she is trying to attract will not flock to her cafe just because the hamburgers have a reputation of being costly. It is a different story entirely if her burgers are indeed the best hamburgers in the region, but if her only marketing ploy is to inflate the price and spread the word that her café caters to the tastes of the affluent, she does not have a good chance of succeeding in her restaurant venture.

Is marketing valuable? Absolutely. Can marketing increase your sales if it is done correctly? Absolutely. Will marketing save your company if your product is subpar or if your services are lacking? No. There is little chance that marketing can be effective in this situation. If you believe in your product or service and you know there is a market among the affluent for what you have to offer, you should absolutely devise a marketing campaign that will garner attention because an effective marketing campaign can truly increase your sales.

Why is marketing to the affluent unique?

Why is it that traditional marketing efforts such as print ads and billboards work while trying to get the attention of affluent customers? Is there any reason why you should not try a one-size-fits all approach when crafting your marketing methods? The answer is simple: Affluent people share many commonalities with people from other income levels in regard to some marketing methods, but if you really want to target affluent people as a primary customer base, you will need to use techniques that appeal specifically to the affluent.

Commonalities

Broad marketing tactics can work for a variety of markets. Provide free samples to a customer and, regardless of that customer's economic status, an opinion will be formed about the product. The hope is that the person sampling the product will think highly of the product and be compelled to make a purchase. The marketing tactic of making the customer feel special is also universal among all groups of people. If you can make a potential customer feel as though he or she is receiving a special service, you increase your odds of selling your product.

Consider the billboards in Times Square or downtown Los Angeles. They are seen by people from nearly every economic group and must appeal to the highest number of people possible. In most cases, the attempt is just to make people aware of the product, whether it is a new album release by a band or the premiere of a movie. This is simple marketing: Make potential customers aware of the product and hope they will want to buy it.

The difference with affluent people is that they can afford to buy these things. They can download a new music release without giving it much thought. They can take their family to the movies without having to work the outing into a budget. So though these marketing tactics might work on people from many different economic statuses, it is affluent people who can buy these things without hesitation. Smart marketing can create the desire to buy things in nearly anyone, but if a customer simply cannot afford to make the purchase, the marketing campaign might not result in an eventual purchase.

Differences

The techniques used to market to affluent people can be quite different from the techniques used to market to other groups. Although common marketing tactics are often suitable for most demographics, there are certainly some marketing tactics that can be effective specifically for affluent customers.

When marketing to affluent people, you absolutely must present the idea that the purchase experience will be seamless and enjoyable. You already know that affluent people expect excellent customer service, so if possible, this should be an aspect of your marketing strategy. Make it known that your customers are treated exceptionally. Downplay the things that would usually be featured in marketing toward other markets, such as convenient store hours or friendly staff, because affluent customers want more than convenience and friendliness. They want an impeccable shopping experience.

Customers from middle- and lower-class neighborhoods want to know how much a product costs before they consider making the purchase, so a common marketing tactic is to advertise low prices on items. Consider the success of Walmart as a result of its highly advertised "rollback" prices. This tactic is wrong when marketing to affluent customers. Although wealthy customers appreciate a good deal and might negotiate cost when buying a high-ticket item, it is not the rock-bottom prices that lure them in. Advertising something at a drastic reduction can cheapen the value of the item in an affluent customer's mind. A Jaguar dealership advertising drastically reduced prices is probably not going to lure affluent customers in unless the affluent customer had already planned on buying a Jaguar and is looking for a deal.

CASE STUDY:
ADVICE FROM A
MARKETING EXPERT

Stephen Woessner
Marketing expert and author of The
Small Business Owner's Handbook to
Search Engine Optimization

If your target audience is an affluent one, that should be your only audience. Small-business owners might say they want to market to affluent customers, but they often find that they do not have the chutzpah and begin selling everything to everyone and offering discounted items and coupons. Suppose a small-business owner wants to open a flower shop and target affluent customers. If an affluent buyer is looking for new, unique, hybrid flowers and is willing to pay $100 per dozen, he or she does not want to see the flower shop having a dozen-rose blowout sale at $9.99. The flower shop owner has to decide whether the shop will sell thousands of bouquets at discounted prices or instead sell several hundred dozen unique flowers that can only be found during a certain season. The shop owner has to decide whether he or she wants to market to affluent customers or mainstream customers. Then, the shop owner has to decide which types of products or species of flowers or hybrids to offer from a product selections standpoint and rely on industry experts to profile affluent customers and decide which types of product to stock. The shop owner needs to consider the interior design of the store; nothing can be cheap, and everything must look high end. Correct product positioning to affluent customers will allow for a 5 to 10 percent increase in pricing because the flower shop is selling something unique and different.

Developing a Marketing Plan

If you do not yet have a marketing plan or if you have an old marketing plan and your business needs have since changed, put some effort toward getting a marketing plan down on paper so you have a vision for what your business is going to accomplish.

Unless you are a sole proprietor, there should be several people involved with developing the marketing plan. The person in charge of marketing might not have a keen grasp on what the person in charge of finances or the person managing the employees has in mind for upcoming marketing campaigns. The idea is to ensure all departments are on board and can deliver in the event that the marketing plan is hugely successful.

You already know what your vision for the business is — or, at least, you should know this — so this is not necessarily what will land in your marketing plan. Instead, the marketing plan is more about how you will go about achieving the goals set in your original vision. It will be where you specify if your intention is to solely market to an affluent customer base or if you simply want to include affluent customers as one aspect of your entire marketing base. Do not stop with stating that your intention is to market to wealthy people; state *how* you intend to do so.

When you are composing your marketing plan, consider this an important opportunity to examine the feasibility of what you want to do with your business. Suppose that you do some market research and discover that the single most effective way to get the attention of the wealthy customers within your area is to purchase expensive sponsorship slots for quarterly charitable events hosted by the affluent neighborhood's homeowners association. If your company does not have the financial stability necessary to purchase a sponsorship for these events, you need to examine if other financial liabilities can be reduced in order to afford a sponsorship. If it simply is not possible, your marketing plan will have to revolve around how you intend to grab the attention of the wealthy residents from this neighborhood without sponsoring a charity event and perhaps even how you will eventually get to the point to where down the road you can start sponsoring charitable events.

Prepare to write several drafts of your marketing plan before you settle on something you are comfortable with and that will actually work with your company's needs. Not only will you likely make several revisions before settling on a final draft, but you should also set time aside at least once a year to review your marketing plan and make changes as needed. In an ideal situation, your yearly marketing plan revision will have to make room for your expanding marketing efforts because of your success, but the important thing is to actually revisit the marketing plan and make adjustments as necessary.

If you are at a loss when it comes to conducting market research or composing your marketing plan, consider getting advice from a marketing consultant or perhaps even adding a marketing professional to your team. Although some will claim that adding a marketing professional to a company's roster is too expensive, others will claim that a company cannot afford to not hire a marketing professional.

About Your Customers

If you think a marketing strategy can force consumers to buy something they do not want, research what happened back in the mid-1980s when Coca Cola tried to introduce a product called "New Coke." Despite heavy marketing efforts from the Coca Cola Company, the public was angered by the switch from the taste they had grown accustomed to and rebelled against the product, and the original Coke was reintroduced as a result.

The Federal Trade Commission Act

What do you need to know about the Federal Trade Commission Act? The first thing to know is that you simply cannot make claims in your advertising you cannot back up. Do not make the claim that your product can do something that it cannot, and do not promise services that you cannot (or are not willing to) actually provide. The Act goes beyond these simple concepts and further clarifies that any business or sole proprietor involved in any type of advertising must ensure that no advertising can be misleading or intentionally omit important aspects of the product or service that might influence the customer's purchasing decision.

The Federal Trade Commission (FTC) further states that all advertisements must be "fair," which might seem like a relatively intangible term, but it is something clarified by the Act. The purpose of this clarification is to ensure customers are not misled by an advertisement. The question is whether a typical customer would feel compelled to make a purchase based on the advertisement and whether or not the typical customer would actually receive what he or she expects to receive based on the advertisement. Although it is fine to make the claim that your luxury face cream is preferred by nine out of ten people surveyed as long as you actually have the empirical data to back up the claim, you cannot make the claim wrinkles will disappear overnight by using this cream if you have no research or other proof that this is actually the case. The same principal applies for insinuations appearing in advertisements; you are not allowed to allude to the idea of wrinkles disappearing overnight if you cannot back up the claim with evidence. If your advertisements insinuate something that is not really true — even by accident — you are setting yourself up for an FTC investigation. Imagine the blow to your company's reputation if you became subject to an investigation into deceptive advertising. Avoid this situation altogether by making sure any advertising you use is telling the truth about the product or services you offer.

It also is important to note that the agency responsible for investigating deceptive claims in advertising can vary depending on what product is offered through the advertising and the scope of the advertising. For example, if your ads are for a local audience or for financial services, it might not be the FTC looking into your advertising. Consumers who feel as though your advertising is deceptive might involve local authorities or might contact the Better Business Bureau. Even if no formal investigation comes from these consumer complaints, keep in mind that a complaint about false advertising can destroy your company's reputation. Personal recommendations are golden when dealing with an affluent customer base, so the last thing your company needs is word floating around that you have been making claims you cannot back up in an attempt to trick customers.

About Your Customers

Stay up to date on the latest news from the Federal Trade Commission (www.ftc.gov). It is also a good idea to build up a good reputation through the Better Business Bureau (www.bbb.org).

Traditional Marketing

Marketing has experienced profound changes in the last few years. Although marketing campaigns used to be expensive and it was often difficult to initially realize the effectiveness — or ineffectiveness — of the campaigns, a small business or sole proprietor today can employ a marketing strategy without much investment at all. Even large corporations now use low-cost marketing tactics. Previously, companies often used magazines, newspapers, and direct mail to get coupons in the hands of consumers. Some companies advertised toll-free telephone numbers that consumers had to call in order to request a coupon, which required the company to pay postage charges to mail the consumer the coupon and pay a representative to answer the telephone.

Conversely, if a company wants to give consumers a coupon using today's marketing techniques, it can simply offer a printable coupon on its website, provide the coupon (or coupon code) on its Facebook or Twitter page, or e-mail the coupon to customers who have signed up to receive its free e-newsletter. Not only is this incredibly cost-effective compared to traditional marketing techniques, it is far easier to track the effectiveness of the campaign because everything is electronic. Companies can determine how many people downloaded the coupon compared to how many people actually used the discount, which is something that could only be estimated in the past.

Is traditional marketing obsolete? Although some marketing experts assert that traditional tactics, such as television commercials, print ads, and direct mailing campaigns, are no longer effective, ask this question to parents whose children ask for a toy at the store because they saw it on television. Ask avid readers who read fitness magazines and use coupons for free protein bars whether print ads work. Ask coupon-clippers who fastidiously comb through their mail every day to look for savings whether direct-mail campaigns work. The problem is that they cost quite a bit of money compared to some of the methods being used today. Marketing tactics such as direct mail can also give mixed results; you pay for every advertisement that goes out, yet you cannot be sure the recipients even look at the mailing. Many people toss advertisements directly in the trash without evening opening the envelope. On the other hand, with many Internet advertising methods, you can purchase an ad on a social networking site such as Facebook and only pay a fee when someone actually clicks on the ad.

Your concern regarding traditional marketing should be how it pertains to the affluent population. These tactics, which include billboards or ad placement on public benches, can be highly compartmentalized by the socioeconomic market the campaign is designed to target. The ads presented in economically depressed areas are often different from ads presented within affluent areas, even when the product is the same. Although it is still important to know your target market, if you use new marketing tactics, you might not be able to pinpoint exactly who is viewing your information. For this reason, ensure your advertisements are designed to appeal to your target market, in this case, the affluent demographic.

Choose your marketing mediums carefully. Think about what magazines your target audience reads, where your target market goes, and what they do in their spare time. For example, a print ad in *People Magazine* will probably not reach the people you are trying to reach, but an ad in *The Robb Report* or a regional luxury magazine will reach your intended market. If you plan to place a billboard or other form of advertising in a public place, think carefully about the placement. An ad placed in a program for the local opera house will probably yield more results among the affluent than a billboard placed in an area of town these customers do not generally visit.

Just because you are creating an advertisement does not necessarily mean you will have to break the bank. However, you do need your advertisements to accurately represent the brand of your company. The advertisement must reflect the impression you want your customers to have of your product or service. For example, consider how easy it is to notice which commercials are created in-house for local companies as opposed to companies who paid for their advertising to be produced by advertising companies. If you are selling a sleek new car, you want your ad to be catchy and modern. If you are offering interior decorating services, create your ad with tasteful colors and an eye for design.

If you are offering elegant jewelry, make sure your ads are classic and tastefully designed.

The Changing Definition of Marketing

The face of marketing has changed drastically in the past few years as a result of the Internet and social media. Most customers, whether affluent or otherwise, spend time on the Internet either for business or personal use, and many people have a profile on at least one social media site, such as Facebook, Twitter, or LinkedIn. People use these websites to stay in touch with friends or colleagues, but even as they chat with friends, they are presented with advertisements, many of which appear on the Web page as a result of a computer program that examines the content of their conversations. For example, an online Facebook conversation about yoga might result in ads for local yoga classes or yoga DVDs.

Marketing is moving beyond the simple concept of letting people know about a product. Today, marketing is interactive and is sometimes veiled as something else. BzzAgent (**www.bzzagent. com**) sends free products to prominent members of its target market when members spread the word about a product. House Party (**www.houseparty.com**) sends boxes of items so members can host parties featuring a particular product. Marketing is frequently relying on satisfied customer to spread the news about a product or service all over the globe with the click of a button.

When thinking about marketing, think beyond flyers and television commercials. In order to be successful in today's market, you need to find new ways to get the word out that people like your product or service while still keeping some of the traditional marketing methods in mind.

The basic definition of marketing is the techniques used to sell a product or service, and while this definition is certainly still applicable, the face of marketing continues to evolve. If you have hopes of effectively marketing to affluent customers, you need to not only stay up-to-date with current marketing techniques, but you also need to forecast what marketing trends will be effective for your target market in the future.

Years ago, marketing simply consisted of letting people know about a product. This evolved into letting people know about how wonderful a product is and why customers need to consider buying the product. In the past, marketing tactics were occasionally deceptive by making false claims or promises. Luring customers to a certain product often involved making the product seem greater than it actually was. Deceptive advertising is now against the law within the United States as a result of the Federal Trade Commission Act, mentioned in the previous section.

Marketing then turned to using a wide variety of tactics in order to get customers to open their wallets. Commercials, product placement, and sponsorship of events became the norm. Actors were paid to go out into communities and act as regular people who absolutely loved the product in their hands. These "brand ambassadors" sold more than a product; they sold the idea of a lifestyle that could only be acquired by buying a product.

These tactics are still used today, but they are augmented by viral marketing. Viral marketing uses social websites that are already in existence, such as YouTube and Facebook, in order to sell products. This differs from marketing tactics that use websites owned by the companies producing the advertisement. Consumers are constantly bombarded by advertisements, even if they do not realize it. Although behavioral scientists from different schools of theory vary on their views as to how effective marketing can be if the consumer does not consciously recognize the advertisement, many people assert that sometimes they make purchasing decisions based on a feeling rather than a concrete decision. The quiet marketing tactics used today can be effective.

Social Media and Other Marketing Tools

In the past, a company that wanted to reach customers with an important announcement would compose a letter and send it through the mail or contact the customers individually via telephone. Companies then shifted to disseminating information using e-mail, but all too often, the correspondence was deleted before it was even read. Presently, a company can broadcast news instantaneously using social media outlets. Although this is not a fail-safe method, it is certainly less expensive and does not rely on customers opening a letter or clicking through an e-mail.

About Your Customers

Your customers are probably online, and they want to see what you are doing online, too — as a salesperson and also as a person. Therefore, maintain an impeccable online presence. Do not blog about how much you hate your job or post photos from your drunken weekend in Cancun. If your customers find these things online, you will instantly lose credibility. Affluent people generally do not want to be associated with people who present themselves one way in person but then reveal their true selves online.

What is different about social media websites? If you can compel your customers to your website, you might be able to compel them to "add" or "follow" you on a social media website. If you are unfamiliar with these terms, here is a brief explanation.

- On Facebook and similar social media websites, "adding" someone as a "friend" translates into that person having access to your profile, which is your page on the social media website, and vice versa. Here is an example:

  1. Fred has a Facebook profile he checks regularly and uses to stay in contact with his friends and family.

2. Fred decides he wants to add his favorite sushi bistro as a friend so that he can get notifications about the sushi bistro.

3. The sushi bistro sends out daily notifications through Facebook announcing special deals on food to lure customers in for a meal.

4. Fred sees the notifications and decides he will go to the sushi bistro for lunch because the constant reminders of the food make him hungry.

- On Twitter and similar social media websites, "following" someone means you receive short notifications from that person or company. The messages are not as long as the notifications on Facebook, but links can be provided to direct users to images or websites. Here is an example:

1. Mary has a Twitter account that she primarily checks from her mobile phone.

2. Mary hears that she can get online coupon codes for her favorite clothing boutique by following the store on Twitter, so she "follows" the store.

3. The store periodically "tweets" — the term for sending out a notification via Twitter — about deals and sometimes offers special discounts for Twitter followers.

4. Mary not only uses the Twitter coupons, but this store is the first to come to her mind when she needs to buy a new outfit as a direct result of her continual exposure to the store via Twitter.

What type of Facebook or Twitter posts should you send out? Although you do want to get information out that might make your customers want to buy your product or service, you also want to maintain a tone that makes it seem like you are truly "friends." The following are a few examples to consider:

- **Good:** Come out tomorrow to sample our newest bakery creation: pumpkin spice muffins!

- **Better:** What's cooking in our oven tomorrow? Our newest creation: pumpkin spice muffins! Come on over and try one.

- **Best:** There is just something about the smell of pumpkin spice muffins in the oven! We'll see you tomorrow as we sample this new creation. Be sure to bring some friends.

If this all seems like nonsense to you and you have avoided using social media websites as a means to get the attention of affluent customers because you assume these customers do not waste their time online, think again. According to Ipsos' annual Mendelsohn Affluent Survey, the amount of money a household makes can be directly related to the amount of time the head of the household spends online. The more money a person makes, the more time he or she is likely to spend online.

According to a similar survey mentioned in an article about the Mendelsohn Affluent Survey on ClickZ, more than 14 million affluent customers have smartphones, and 900,000 of them own a tablet computer. The survey also found that search engines such as Google and Bing were the top online destinations visited by affluent users over the past year, followed by social networks, general interest/news, shopping, and travel sites. The affluent are also driving the mobile application market, said the survey. About 38 percent of affluent customers reported that they have downloaded and installed one app, if not more, to their smartphones or wireless devices. Your customer base is online, and if your business is not online, you are missing out.

CASE STUDY: ADVICE FROM A MARKETING EXPERT

Stephen Woessner
Marketing expert and author of
The Small Business Owner's Handbook
to Search Engine Optimization

Social networking allows you to leverage the content on your own website. For example, if you have an interesting post or customer testimonial, you can share it socially, and then it goes "viral." It gives affluent customers an easy way to share that content with people within their circles.

By using social network sites, you can increase your site traffic by 23 percent. The typical conversion rate is 2 to 4 percent of people visiting a website to buy something, which means that 2 to 4 percent of website visitors will make a purchase. On the other hand, if the content on your website is shared socially, the rate increases to 22 percent. That means that instead of a 2 to 4 percent chance of someone making a purchase on your website, the chance has just jumped to 22 percent because something from your website showed up on a social network.

A word of caution: After you have begun using social media websites as a marketing tool, do not rely solely on this tactic for all of your marketing. Social media advertising should only be one of the many tools you use to get your customers' attention. You should have several marketing tactics within your arsenal.

Social media marketing is not perfect; it is a marketing tactic that does come with some risks. When companies begin to use social media marketing, they need to make sure their computers are up-to-date with the latest anti-virus programs. They also need to carefully monitor the Internet to make sure no one else is impersonating the company or representatives of the company. For example, if a company discovers fake coupons circulating online featuring the company's logo and promising a free product or discount, it is up to the company to inform customers the coupons are fake and cannot be redeemed.

Companies that want to have an online presence need to also make sure they can handle any inquiries that come in via the Internet. E-mail should be answered quickly, and social media websites should be patrolled regularly to respond to comments or remove derogatory comments. Using social media as a means of advertising is an active process; customers expect to be able to interact with the company.

Paid advertising via social media

Social media is not exclusively designed for interacting with your customers in a casual way. These websites also allow for more traditional methods of advertising, which allows you to combine new and old marketing tactics. Facebook provides an excellent example; business owners can create Facebook profiles and interact with their customers using the social media platform, but they can also purchase ads that will appear on users' sidebars.

The technology used to decide which users get to see your ad is actually quite sophisticated. If you own a small boutique in San Diego and do not offer services outside of your physical location, your ad will not show up on the sidebar of a Facebook user in Detroit. The technology behind these ads can also specify what type of people you want your ads to reach. For example, suppose you specialize in designing luxury baby-seat covers and you want your ad to reach young mothers. You can set your preferences so the ad only shows up on the sidebar of women who fall within a certain age range and within a certain geographic location. Best of all, the only time you pay for the ad is when people actually click on the ad, which leads them to your Facebook page or website. Of course, there is no guarantee that arriving at your website will compel a visitor to buy something, but this can be a cost-effective way to get noticed by the demographic you are trying to reach.

Why has the face of marketing changed? It has changed because culture has changed. Information is instantaneous and constant. When an affluent customer wants information about a product or service, he or she fully expects to immediately find that information by using a computer or mobile phone. Suppose Sue chats with a friend who tells her about a bakery for pet treats, but her friend does not know the name or location of the bakery because she has only heard about it from other people. Sue's expectation is that she can type the phrase "bakery for pets" into a search engine on her mobile phone's browser and immediately find the name of the bakery, the location and hours, and written reviews from a variety of customers. If she cannot find this information, she might assume that the bakery simply does not exist, which is not an impression you want your affluent customers to believe.

The way information is presented in advertisements to potential and existing customers has also changed. Review print ads from around the 1950s compared to present day, and one thing is glaringly obvious: people want their information in a quick, easy-to-read format. The Internet has changed the way people read. Bullet points, changing fonts, and quick phrases will grab attention quicker than a huge block of text. In the past, advertisements for products such as kitchen cleaners were page long descriptions of the benefits of the product and the perils of not using the product. In the present day, a long advertisement like this would likely be disregarded by most customers, particularly affluent customers who have limited time to waste on reading through flowery imagery about kitchen cleaners. Images now take the predominant position in most advertisements instead of big blocks of text, although there are certainly exceptions to this trend.

Your website

If you do not yet have an actual website for your business, put it on your list of important tasks to tackle. Affluent customers seek out information online just like other customers do, but your wealthy customers might lose patience if they do not quickly find exactly what they are looking for. Not only should you have a website, but you should have one that is designed with affluent customers in mind.

You should not aim to entertain your customers online but instead should aim to provide clear, concise information and provide an easy way for your online customers to get what they are looking for. According to *The Art of Selling to the Affluent* by Matt Oechsli, wealthy customers are not looking for flashy graphics or silly entertainment when they go to a merchant's website. Instead, they want information presented in a way that is simple to navigate and gets right to the point. This does not mean that affluent people are not technologically savvy; remember that even people who understand the intricate interworking of a computer and the Internet do not want to wait for a website to load because of a huge photo or graphic. When an affluent customer lands on your website, it is probably because he or she is looking for specific information, and as a result, you should make it as simple as possible for visitors to find that information.

Your website should also include an easy way for visitors to contact you if they cannot find the information they are looking for or if they have a question that is not answered on the website. Whether that means you put a link to send an e-mail to on the website, or if you enable the website with a live-chat feature so prospective customers can get their questions answered instantly in a live-chat format, the point is to give them a quick and easy format that enables them to get the information they are looking for. Otherwise, they might get frustrated with the whole process and decide to either not make the purchase or to find a different merchant to make the purchase from. Affluent customers do not want to have their time wasted, and not just in their face-to-face dealings.

Make your website as aesthetically pleasing as possible without sacrificing functionality. If a few less photographs allow your website to run faster, consider only placing vital photographs on the website. This does not mean you should present a website that is boring, with only essential text and nothing else. You might have to pay a little more money to have a nicer website, but this added expense should be considered to be an investment in your business. Steer clear of "free" websites that are heavily sponsored by ads, which means the website is free for you but your online visitors are assaulted by a steady stream of advertisements when they visit.

If you do not have experience in creating a website, or if you simply do not have the time to tackle this task, consider hiring a professional website developer to do the job for you. A good website developer can create something that is not only functional but is different from all of the other websites that have been created from standard templates. You want your website to stick out among the rest as something that is special and ahead of its time because this is also the image you want your business to convey. Remember, your website is a reflection of your business and is also a reflection of you as a businessperson. What does your website say about you? If it is cheaply thrown together and difficult to navigate, you might find that potential customers decide that you are difficult to deal with, even before they actually meet you. Make sure the website is an accurate reflection of the product or service you offer, too. You would not want a flowery motif on a website for a sports car dealership, just like you would not want a sleek, metallic theme on a website for a classic flower shop. Strive for continuity of the image you want to portray throughout your website.

CASE STUDY: ADVICE FROM A MARKETING EXPERT

Eric S. English
Senior Web Developer
Innovate Web Development
www.innovatewebdevelopment.com/
main.shtml

Different websites have varying degrees of credibility. If a visitor visits a home page and it has a lot of advertisements and banners flashing, the credibility level will be low. It also demonstrates that it was probably a free website. It might indicate that the website has few visitors or something like that. At the very least, this demonstrates that the owner of the website has to generate income through advertisements in order to afford the website.

Whether you should pay someone to create your website for you really depends on what you are looking for. One thing that is important is something called "User Interaction Psychology." Only a professional would be able to test for that sort of thing. User Interaction Psychology relates to how any individual user looks at the screen and where his or her eyes are moving. Information like this gives a professional website designer important information, so the professional can create the design and build the website according to that information. There are so many things like User Interaction Psychology and other factors that the average person does not think about. A person who has a little experience can create a website, but there are just so many avenues that professionals have available to them that the amateurs do not have.

Some people do not use professional website designers because of the initial cost involved. One thing people do not realize is that typically you do not have a lot of ongoing fees. Some people are surprised by the up-front expense of a website, but what they don't realize is that this is typically the only expense that they will have with the exception of hosting. Hosting typically costs around $100-$150 a year, but hosting is really the only recurring fees unless the website uses Web mastering or maintenance. A website is an investment.

The website is up 24 hours, it has international capabilities, and depending on what type of professional you get, you might be optimized for search engines. This allows your website to be found easier all over the world, which is another thing amateurs cannot do.

The Internet changes; even how you create a website changes. A professional can create from a code level, not just by putting images together to create a website from a template. Also, the professional can create a website in such a way that allows flexibility in the website and allow for future changes.

Other marketing mediums

Internet marketing goes beyond the World Wide Web. Consider the functionality of the cell phones your customers carry. Long gone are the days when these phones were used solely for making calls; people can now surf the Internet, manage their schedules, and send e-mail using their phones. Even if your customers do not use all of the features offered on the cell phones on the market now, there is a good chance they are at least using texting features and might even participate in QR codes to obtain discounts on their phones.

Texting Discounts

Some merchants text discounts directly to customers using their cell phones. Common promotions include things along the lines of "Use coupon code HAPPY to save $20 on tickets to tonight's show," or "Show this text at the register and enjoy 30% off your purchase."

Although these promotions can be quite effective in some instances, be careful when using this method with affluent customers. Remember that wealthy customers are typically quite busy and do not like to be disturbed throughout the day with unexpected interruptions. When a text is received, this usually prompts a person to stop whatever he or she is doing to look at the text to make sure it is not something that needs to be acted upon immediately. If the recipient perceives the unsolicited text as an annoyance, some damage might have been done with regards to how the customer views the sender. Disturb an existing customer in the middle of a busy business day with a text that does not have any benefit to the customer, and you might have one less customer.

How can you make sure that texts are used in a positive way instead of being an annoyance to your customers? There are a few different things to keep in mind with regards to texting customers:

- Do not send unsolicited texts. The people who receive your texts should be people who are already familiar with your service or product and who have expressed an interest in receiving texts from you. It is a horrible idea to send an unsolicited text to an affluent customer you do not already have a relationship with. Skimming through the phone directory and sending random texts will result in some angry people who will probably vow to never use your product or service because of your unsolicited texts.

- Do not send texts to all of your customers. You need to get permission from your customers to send texts, and this means providing your customers the opportunity to sign up for text notifications of sales or deals.

- Do not hide the fact that you intend to text your customers; do not put small print at the bottom of every contract that says something along the lines of "Providing us with your telephone number indicates an acceptance of occasional texts with discount offers." Affluent customers will not appreciate being tricked into granting permission for unsolicited cell phone interruptions without realizing they granted permission in the first place.

- Do not text frequently. It is highly unlikely that your customers want a daily update from you about the "Smoothie of the Day" or whatever else it is you offer, at least not in a text format. Information that is appropriate for daily dissemination is more appropriate for a Facebook or Twitter page or perhaps even in an e-mail format if the customer has signed up to received this information. Do not assault your customers with information every single day, especially if the information is not really a benefit to them.

- Reserve texts for special offers or information. Are you offering a significant discount on your product or service for a limited time? Has a highly anticipated product finally arrived and is ready for purchase? These are the types of notifications that customers will not mind receiving, as long as they are not frequent and have a true value to the customer. You want your customers to be excited when they realize they have a text from you because this usually means you have something special to offer. Strive to make your texts of real benefit to the recipients instead of using texts as a way to keep reminding your customers you are still around and open for business.

- Do not use texts as a means of personal communication unless your customer has given you permission to do so. Suppose a customer has expressed interest in purchasing an expensive luxury item from you that you have to special order and will take a couple weeks to receive. You work closely with the customer to find out exactly what he or she wants, and the customer spends a great deal of money on the product. When the product arrives in your office and is ready for delivery, an impersonal text to the customer stating the product has arrived might seem insulting to the customer. He or she might get angry about this method of notification and might think, "I spent so much money on this product, and spent so much time with this merchant, and all I get is a quick text to tell me the product is ready?" Do not allow the convenience of texting to lure you into inadvertently insulting your affluent customers.

- Spell check your texts more than once. Texting does not allow for a lot of space for what you want to say, but this does not mean you do not need to make sure the information you are preparing to text is spelled correctly and is grammatically correct. Many texting programs include a spell-checker, but they also feature auto-correct capabilities, which can result in some embarrassing mistakes. Imagine if you type out a text for your customers that says, "Come see our new line of handbags!" but you accidentally misspell "see," which is auto-corrected by your text program into "sex." This means you have just sent a mass text out to a large group of affluent customers urging them to "Come sex our new line of handbags!" Read and reread your texts before you send them out, and if possible, get another person to review the text before it is sent out. It is important to remember that every bit of information you send out on behalf of your business is a direct representation of who you are and what your business represents, even if the information is two lines long.

- Avoid texting shortcuts like "BRB" for "be right back" or "LOL" for "laughing out loud." You might consider these as clever ways to reduce the number of characters you send, but imagine how frustrating this can be to someone who is not fluent in text talk. Send a text to a customer that says "2moro doesn't have 2b ADAD b/c new Jimmy Choos are in, NISM?" and there is a good chance that you will confuse the majority of your recipients. You know that your intended message was this: "Tomorrow doesn't have to be 'another day another dollar' because new Jimmy Choos are in, need I say more?" But to your customers, it might look like a text sent by a drunken person.

- Make sure you know the capabilities of your texting program before using this method for getting information out to customers. Listing too many recipients on a text might result in the information not getting to the customers in a timely manner, and some customers might not get the text at all. If you send out notification of a lunchtime special giving free appetizers to everyone who mentions the text, but the majority of your customers do not receive the text until far past lunchtime, your customers might feel as though they have been deprived of something exclusive, which generally does not bode well among the affluent.

- If a customer wants to be removed from your text database, do so promptly. Suppose a customer casually mentions she would like to be removed, but you forget to remove her and she winds up getting more texts from you. What does this say to this customer? Not only does it say you did not truly listen to what she had said, but it also says you do not genuinely care about your customers' preferences. This is not an image you want to convey to your affluent customers. For this reason, do not make your customers jump through hoops to get removed from your texting list. Trying to trick your customers into staying on a marketing list they want to be removed from will not result in them resigning to receive these texts and eventually make a purchase from you. Instead, it is going to make them angry.

Take care when using texting as a method to bring customers into your business or when conveying important information to customers. Although texting might seem like the simplest way to get brief information into the hands of your target audience, it is certainly not a perfect method and might not be appropriate based on your customers. You need to know your customers and understand if they are the type of people to welcome text communication before using texting as a means of communication.

QR code discounts

A Quick Response code, most commonly referred to as a QR code, is an image scanned by a smart phone and used to convey information. You can find QR codes on advertisements; they look like squares with blotchy designs inside. Scanning the QR code gives the user more information or a special discount. Airlines use QR codes as a way of allowing customers to retain their boarding pass on their smart phones as opposed to carrying around a printed version. Instead of handing the boarding agent a paper boarding pass, the user simply presents the smart phone with the QR code on the screen and is checked in for the flight. Merchants place QR codes on their print advertisements, which shoppers scan with their phones and then present to the merchant for a special discount offered only to the people with this tool. Although not everyone is using this technology, there is a good chance that this method rapidly will become mainstream. For this reason, it is a good idea to understand how these codes work and how you can use them to convey important information to your affluent customers.

About Your Customers

Create your own QR code using online tools, such as those offered by http://qrcode.kaywa.com.

Use a QR code to provide important information about your product or service at a quick glance. You can also use these codes to provide your customers with special discounts or free offers. Not all of your customers will use your QR code, and in fact, some of them will not even understand what the blotchy image is for to begin with. The reason why you want to offer a QR code for your business is simple: some of your affluent customers will expect you to. They have grown accustomed to using QR codes with other merchants, and if you do not provide this option, there is a chance these customers will consider you behind the times.

The QR code does not have to offer a discount or point the customer toward a special sale. You can also use these codes to convey information about your product. For example, if you offer a specialized product that generally requires a great deal of explanation before a customer will make a purchase, consider placing a QR code on your business card. The QR code provides the potential customer with everything he or she needs to know about your product with a simple scanning of the code using a smart phone. This is far easier than suggesting customers visit the FAQ on your website because the customer does not have to take the time to sit down in front of a computer and type in your website address. Instead, your customer gets instant access to answers to all his or her questions about your product with a simple scan of the QR code. As this technology becomes more widely available, do not be surprised if consumers — affluent and otherwise — expect to encounter QR codes whenever dealing with a merchant.

E-mail

There is a good chance your wealthy customers have cell phones that allow them to receive and respond to e-mail. Regardless of if they use their phones for this or if they only check e-mail when sitting in front of their computers, consider how e-mail can help you communicate with your customers.

Many of the same rules that apply to using texts for your business apply to using e-mail, as well. Always use a spell-checker and make sure your grammar is appropriate before hitting the send button. Do not deluge your customers with a high number of e-mail, and always honor your customers' wishes if they express a desire to be removed from your e-mail list. Also, remember to keep your e-mail list private; do not allow e-mail recipients to see who else received your mass e-mail because this is a breach of privacy that allows anyone receiving the e-mail to send another e-mail to any of the other recipients. Solve this problem by selecting "BCC" when inserting e-mail addresses into mass e-mail. "BCC" stands for "blind courtesy copy" and keeps recipients from seeing who else the communication was sent to.

E-mail should be your primary form of communication with your wealthy customers only if they have expressed an interest in having this as the main form of communication. Most affluent customers still expect to receive a telephone call if there is something important they need to know. What qualifies as "important" with regards to communicating with customers? A great example is if a customer has asked you to find out the answer to a question about a product during a previous conversation. If the conversation took place via e-mail, and if you know this is the customer's preferred method of communication, it is appropriate to e-mail the answer to the customer when you find out what he or she is looking for. If the conversation was face-to-face, but the customer added that you should simply e-mail the answer when you have it, e-mail is appropriate in this situation as well because that is clearly what the customer wants. On the other hand, if the original conversation when the request took place was face-to-face, and your customer said something along the lines of "Let me know when you find out the answer," this indicates a need for a telephone call as opposed to e-mail. It is completely appropriate in the event that you reach your customer's voice mail to say something along the lines of, "I found out the information you were looking for; I am e-mailing the specifics to you right now," as long as you do indeed send the e-mail promptly. Be sure to also add that the customer is welcome to call you for further clarification, and it is also a good idea to make a follow-up phone call later if the customer has not responded to your phone call or e-mail.

Every communication you have with your customers is a form of marketing. Something as simple as a quick reply to a customer's e-mail is a form of marketing because you convey a variety of things through this method.

- Do you respond promptly? If so, this shows you do business efficiently and also pay attention to the needs of your customers.

- Do you respond in an eloquent way with an appealing writing style? Wealthy customers are often quite educated and will immediately recognize bad writing.

- Do you respond with the answer to the customer's question? If you try to dance around the fact you really do not have the answer to the customer's question and do not offer any real solution to what the customer wants, this will be glaringly obvious.

- Do you sound polite? E-mail can be a tricky form of communication because there is no way to hear intended voice inflections that can completely change the meaning of sentences.

As with any form of communication to a customer, make sure your point gets across in a professional and friendly way that makes the customer want to deal with you in the future. If possible, have someone else look over your e-mail before you send it out, though this is not always feasible in situations when you are dealing with a high number of e-mail on a daily basis.

About Your Customers

"Spam" refers to e-mail that is unsolicited and is of no value to the recipient. If your e-mail gets flagged as spam, your potential customers will probably never even see it because the e-mail will go directly to junk e-mail folders. Do not allow your e-mail communications to look "spammy."

Unsolicited e-mail sent as advertisements to affluent customers should still try to look as though it is personalized. Put the customer's name in the e-mail, and do not fill the e-mail with images and logos because otherwise the recipient might have a difficult time loading the e-mail or might encounter error messages. You do not want your business affiliated with e-mail that will not open properly. Also, think carefully about what the subject line of the e-mail will to say before you send it. Most affluent customers will skip right past any e-mail that has a subject line riddled with asterisks and wording that makes the product being offered seem cheap. Spelling errors in the subject line make the e-mail look like spam, and even if you have an existing relationship with a customer, the e-mail might wind up deleted and unread.

- Bad subject line:
  *****CLOSE-OUT ON CLEARANCE ITEMS!!!!!!******

- Good subject line:
  Exclusive Offer for Mrs. Helen Witherspoon

Although the first subject line listed above might grab the attention of an average shopper who is mostly concerned about the cost of items, it is the second example of a subject line that is most likely to catch the eye of an affluent customer. Not only does it include the recipient's title and name in the subject line, but it also offers information in a dignified way. The first example appears to be virtually screaming at the recipient, whereas the second example indicates the information contained within the e-mail is of an exclusive nature.

Of course, it takes more than an eye-catching subject line for e-mail to grab an affluent customer's attention. You have to offer information the customer actually wants. It might be that the customer does not know he or she wants the information until receiving the e-mail, but these communications should provide information that compels the potential customer to want to learn more. Present the information in such a way that suggests the information is not readily available to everyone and that the person receiving the e-mail is privy to something special. You also need to make sure you have easy and specific instructions listed at the bottom of the e-mail that invites people to unsubscribe if they no longer want to receive it. Although it might be difficult to realize that not everyone wants to receive your e-mail, it would be far worse to continue to annoy your potential customers (and existing customers) with e-mail they really do not want. Even worse would be disregarding their requests to stop the e-mail because at this point you are being disrespectful. Affluent customers expect — and usually receive — respect from the merchants they choose to deal with. If you are not respectful in your dealings with these customers, they will not only delete e-mail from you, but they will quickly find a merchant who is willing to cater to their preferences, which may mean no unsolicited e-mail communication.

SEO explained

You will undoubtedly encounter the term "SEO" repeatedly when researching marketing online. Although there are many facets to this topic, it is possible to explain the overall concept easily so you will understand how it can be used in your business.

SEO is the acronym for search engine optimization. A search engine is the online tool a consumer uses to search for information online; examples of search engines include Google and Bing. People use search engines to find all types of information online.

Whether it is a new car or an old high school sweetheart, an Internet search typically begins with a search engine.

When people use search engines, they input keywords in an effort to find what they are looking for. For example, if you lived in Tampa and you wanted to buy a Mercedes, you would type "buy a Mercedes in Tampa" into a search engine. The search engine will then quickly search for websites that are about Mercedes vehicles for sale within the Tampa area and list those websites that match this description. The websites listed first on the results page are the closest match to the keywords being searched for based on several factors, including how reliable the search engine deems the website and, perhaps most importantly, whether the website paid for a premium spot as a sponsored link.

Search engines remember keywords that are searched for by Internet users. For example, website owners can use a program called NicheBot to find out which keywords Internet users are searching for and with what approximate frequency. Why is this important? If website owners can find out what people are looking for online, the website owners can make sure their websites feature this information. A car dealer in Tampa can track how many people are looking for high-end vehicles online based on the information presented by these analytical tools.

SEO involves finding out which keywords Internet users are looking for and integrating these words into one's website. Websites use SEO information to provide the information people are looking for, while also potentially moving a website up higher on a search engine results page. A website at the top of a search engine's results page has a much better chance of being clicked than a website that does not make its appearance until three or four pages into the search results.

You do not have to rely on complicated Internet tools to tell you where your website falls within a search engine's results. Simply go to a search engine and type in the phrases that a potential customer would type in when searching for what you offer. For example, if you specialize in refurbishing antique furniture, type the phrase "antique furniture refurbishing in (your location)." Look to see where your website comes up on the list of results. If you are not even on the first page of the results, this tells you a few things. Either you have a great deal of competition from other antique furniture refurbishing professionals within your area, or your website is not showing up on the top results for another reason. It might be time to revamp your website to make it more compatible with search engines, which is something for which you might want to consult a professional web developer. You might also want to consider buying a sponsorship with the search engine, which costs money but generally results in your website landing among the top results from the search. Why should you care where your website lands on the results page from an online search? The answer is simple: many people searching for something specific online will not bother to scroll down or even go to the second page of results. They assume that the most appropriate results appear at the top of the first page.

Affluent customers do not want to spend a great deal of time sifting through results on a search engine. They want to quickly visit the top website offering the information they are looking for. SEO is just one of the tools that can be used to ensure your website is one of the top results in an Internet search, and this is what makes SEO so important to a business owner. SEO makes your website content appear pertinent to search engines without appearing "spammy." A website appears spammy if it has the same words mentioned excessively because this looks like a blatant attempt at getting search engines to list it near the top of the results page. For example, a website might make the repeated claims of having the "best selection of handmade jewelry in San Antonio" so many times that it looks unnatural and forced, and this is when the website falls into the realm of looking spammy.

CASE STUDY:
ADVICE FROM A
MARKETING EXPERT

Stephen Woessner
Marketing expert and author of
The Small Business Owner's Handbook
to Search Engine Optimization

With social networking websites, you can assume more than 50 percent of their membership falls into what I would consider above average incomes; for example, 58.7 percent of LinkedIn members have an income of $100K or more, and 50 percent of Twitters members have an income of $60K or more. These are not necessarily what you would consider affluent, but most of these buyers have more disposable income and are the ones who you want to approach and sell to. When you think of the total audience within social networking websites, there are significant numbers of people making a fairly decent living. Affluent audiences are online, but they are also actively engaged in one of today's most efficient online marketing strategies — social networking.

Marketing tactics relating to how you distribute information (e-mail, SEO, social, pay per click, etc.) will be fundamentally the same for affluent customers. You want to SEO your content, run an e-mail campaign, implement a social network strategy, and conduct publicity that links back to your website. Fundamentally, the tactics are the same, but the difference is the content and the messaging and being able to position yourself. It is difficult to sell to an affluent audience if that is not where you come from and do not understand the market. It is hard to be the person selling Bentleys when you drive a beat-up Accord. The way potential customers measure credibility is through the message and what your content says. It is through credibility indicators.

This is where one of my favorite authors, Timothy Ferriss in *The 4-Hour Workweek*, does a great job explaining how to establish credibility indicators. For example, I have more credibility trying to approach *The New York Times* or *The Wall Street Journal* because I was featured in *Inc.* magazine in July; before that, it would have been difficult. If you are going to go after an affluent audience, you need to speak that language. You need to study the market and understand what indicators to add to your message for it to be acceptable. By doing this, you will not seem like you are a Walmart brand trying to sell Bentleys.

Small-business owners tend to talk about the things that are unique but that no one cares about. So, my suggestion is to ensure you are speaking the language affluent customers care about and not so much about the tactics you are using.

Marketing efforts

Learning about what has worked for other companies can help you in your marketing efforts, but marketing techniques you design on your own can work as well, even if they have not been tested or proven. If you truly know your customers, you have insight that other marketing experts do not. Your customers will become more than a demographic for you and you will view them as real people with genuine interests and needs. This is one of the keys of marketing to the affluent: remembering that they are individuals and not one lump group that can be easily swooned into buying a product or service.

Some of the best marketing campaigns were effective because they put a face to a brand. Consider the Marlboro Man; he became the human representative of a company. Marlboro was not just a cigarette; it was also part of a rugged, manly lifestyle. Many men turned to these cigarettes because of what the Marlboro Man campaign essentially said to consumers: This is what a real man looks like. If you do not smoke Marlboro cigarettes, you are not a real man.

Will marketing campaigns like these work for affluent customers. The answer is a not-so-definitive maybe. Much depends on what lifestyle you are trying to sell. Suppose you are selling organic fruit drinks. Appealing to most people's innate desire to be healthy might work by presenting a representative who is the pinnacle of health, but today, many people do not buy into fictional characters as authentic representations of a product. Unless there is something about the representative that catches an affluent person's attention, there is a good chance the entire ad campaign will simply be dismissed as yet another advertisement.

You can fix the problem by appealing specifically to affluent people. One way to do this is by marketing the organic fruit drinks as something not widely available. Market the drinks as being comprised of exotic fruits, and make it clear that these drinks are only for the most discerning customers who truly care about how they look and feel. Your fruit drink will appeal to affluent customers more if they think that not everyone has access to these drinks and that the drinks are more beneficial than drinks commonly found on store shelves. Of course, do not market a drink as tasty if it has a pungent taste, and do not market the drink as exotic if it is only comprised of Valencia oranges and Washington apples. You must offer a quality product if you have hopes of succeeding.

One of the best ways to market your fruit drink is to find a way to get the drink into the hands of the movers and shakers. This could mean stocking the backstage area of a huge concert venue with the drink so when the famous singer leaves the arena, he or she does so with your fruit drink in hand. In theory, this is a great way to get your product into the hands of a celebrity, but if you do not have a contract with the singer to appear with your drink, he or she might just guzzle the drink backstage and no one will ever see him or her with it. On the other hand, it can be an effective tactic if the celebrity decides he or she likes your drink. Consider all the times Britney Spears or Rachel Zoe was photographed drinking Starbucks® coffee. These moments happened because the celebrities had access to and liked the drink, and as a result, other affluent people identified with these celebrities and stopped in for a coffee, as well.

If your marketing budget does not allow you to stock concert venues or get a contract with a celebrity, start smaller but with the same concept. For example, ask the most elite fitness center in your area if you can come in on a busy day and offer free samples of your fruit drink to people as they leave. You will be meeting a need because people are usually thirsty after a workout, and you will get your product into the hands of people to whom you are trying to market your product. Affluent people are not above taking free samples, especially if the free sample is something they want to try. If your fruit drink is indeed tasty and you can get people to try it, you have a good chance at creating a demand for your product.

Do not be afraid to market something as luxurious if it actually merits this distinction. Consider the famous marketing campaign by De Beers, "A Diamond is Forever," which was coined in 1947. Consider the many different layers to the statement:

1. Diamonds are of high quality.

2. Diamonds are indicative of eternity.

3. Men who buy diamonds for their wives are giving a gift that will last forever.

4. An engagement ring signifies the future, just as a diamond signifies eternity.

It is quite a tall order to say so many things with so few words, but De Beers was able to craft just the right marketing campaign to tell consumers that the only acceptable way to properly secure a future with a girlfriend is to propose with a diamond.

If there are luxurious aspects to your product or service, say so. Capitalize on the luxury aspect of what you have to offer if your hope is to get the attention of affluent customers. Most wealthy customers seek out luxury in their purchases, so if you can set your product apart by marketing it as special and luxurious, you might catch the attention of your target market.

An excellent example of ad campaigns that were designed to make customers feel as though a product would make them feel special were the various campaigns American Express has presented over the years. From "Do you know me?" to "Membership has its privileges," this credit card company has always conveyed an image of prestige and status. Although it is true that there are versions of the American Express card that are available to the general public, the platinum and "black cards" from American Express are considered quite prestigious. In fact, in order to obtain a Centurion Card, which is the infamous American Express black card, a customer must receive an invitation to apply, and when accepted, he or she receives a boxed kit that welcomes the cardholder to a new world of credit card usage. Of course, the customer service received by members who have these cards is absolutely impeccable, which might be a factor more important to the cardholders than the extremely high credit limits that are available. Beyond all these factors, however, the prestige that comes with these cards is what truly lures many of the customers to accept the invitation, despite the high annual fee that accompanies one of these accounts.

Try to think of what would appeal to you if money were no object. Where would you shop? What would you buy? More important, what would someone have to say or do in order to get you to open your wallet? If you can put yourself into the same mind-set as someone who has money to spend, you have a much better chance of effectively marketing to the affluent.

A Comprehensive Marketing Plan

Traditional marketing methods should not be immediately disregarded as outdated, just as newer versions of marketing should not be dismissed as too trendy. Ideally, your marketing tactics will combine older and newer marketing tactics to create a comprehensive marketing plan that reaches the customers you want to target.

Pay close attention to what works for your particular offerings. Experiment with a variety of marketing tactics and adjust as necessary. You might be pleasantly surprised to find that something you thought would not really work turns out to be quite successful, such as a direct-letter campaign, sponsoring a private school's talent show, or a Twitter campaign. There is no rule that says old marketing tactics are "out" and new marketing tactics are "in," particularly when dealing with an affluent audience. These customers expect to be courted. If you expect to grab the attention of wealthy customers with an occasional form e-mail, you decrease your chances of success.

Chapter 5

Sink, Swim, or Sell

> *"You've got to be success minded. You've got to feel that things are coming your way when you're out selling; otherwise, you won't be able to sell anything."*
>
> Benjamin Jowett, English scholar

S uppose you spend a great deal of effort developing your marketing plan. You tirelessly court affluent customers in an attempt to get their attention and gain their trust. Your marketing techniques are as perfect as you can make them for your target market, and as a result, you are actually luring people into your place of business. Even better, these people are prepared to make purchases.

What happens next? Despite your amazing marketing efforts, this entire scenario has the potential to go awry if customers walk into your place of business and are greeted with anything less than perfect customer service. Suppose you have aggressively marketed toward an affluent audience by promising them goods or services that will exceed their expectations and enrich their lives. These affluent customers walk into your place of business and are greeted by a lukewarm "Hey" from a bored and inexperienced salesperson or, worse yet, are not greeted at all. Equally frustrating for an affluent customer would be to take the time to visit your website only to find the page takes a significant amount of time to load, there are misspellings present within the website's text, or the pictures on the website are fuzzy. If your website is dazzling but does not feature clear indicators as to how to actually make a purchase or schedule an appointment for a service, affluent customers might just click away from your website instead of pursuing a purchase by making a phone call to your office or sending an e-mail message.

It boils down to this: You can market like a pro, but if your sales techniques are ineffective, customers will not make the purchase. Affluent customers not only expect to be courted for their business, they also expect to receive impeccable customer service.

The Sales Experience

You already know that effective marketing efforts intended to appeal directly to affluent customers can be one of the best ways to initially get the attention of the wealthy population. It is also important to remember that the process of getting affluent customers does not end with the customer walking into your place of business or clicking on your website. Just because you have piqued the interest of an affluent customer does not guarantee that the sale is a done deal.

Although most business owners wholeheartedly agree that it is of the utmost importance to treat all potential customers with respect while trying to get a sale, the need for demonstrating respect increases exponentially when dealing with an affluent customer base. Affluent customers expect the best customer service when buying products or services and have probably become accustomed to receiving the best customer service from other retailers and service providers. If you provide anything less than impeccable customer service to affluent customers, you will likely not make the sale.

The sales experience you present to your affluent customers should be one that not only caters to their needs, it should also anticipate those needs. An effective salesperson builds rapport with customers that allows the salesperson to anticipate when a sale might be imminent. Using the example of the flower shop mentioned in the previous chapter, consider these three scenarios:

1. Tina the flower shop owner knows that high school graduation is coming, so she sends out a coupon through the mail and through e-mail for a discount on flowers. She hopes that this will remind her affluent customers that flowers are great gifts for graduates. She also is anticipating that some of her customers might want some flowers as graduation party decorations.

2. Frank the flower shop owner anticipates high school graduation every year with a telephone campaign that involves calling all of his customers to ask whether they need flowers during the graduation season. It takes him a significant amount of time to call every customer, but some of the customers seem receptive and order flowers during the phone calls.

3. Erin the flower shop owner plans far in advance for the graduation season. This owner already knows which customers will likely need flowers for graduation parties and other celebratory events surrounding graduation because she knows which of her clients have children, friends, and other loved ones who will be graduating. Instead of calling every single client, she sends a small bouquet to affluent customers who need flowers during the graduation season and also includes a personalized note with the flowers congratulating the clients for their upcoming celebrations. If this does not prompt the clients to order additional flowers, Erin then takes the time to call the clients

to congratulate them again on the upcoming celebrations and asks what she can do to help them with their flower needs. She might also propose some special arrangements based on the individual needs of each customer, such as proposing particular flowers for an arrangement based on the graduate's preferences, which, if Erin is a highly effective flower shop owner, she will already know.

Each of these owners has the right idea by anticipating the upcoming graduation season, and each of them has planned marketing techniques to try to drum up business. When that marketing is combined with effective selling techniques, the entire methodology becomes effective for an affluent audience.

Tina anticipates the graduation season, but while her mail and e-mail campaign might help put the idea of purchasing flowers into the minds of her customers, the campaign lacks personalization, which might prompt recipients to simply toss the mail into the trash or delete the e-mail. Sending out discount coupons to affluent customers can backfire if not done correctly. These customers do not want a random coupon to show up within their mail; they want their flower providers to anticipate their needs instead of simply sending out discount coupons to everyone.

Frank's idea to contact his clients is a better idea, but his methodology is rather time-consuming. He might also prove to be an annoyance to his clients if they have no need for graduation flowers. Not many customers appreciate unsolicited phone calls asking them to open their wallets — affluent or not. By calling customers at random, Frank is sending the following message: "I have no idea whether you have a need for graduation flowers because I do not know or care about you or your situation. I am willing to disregard the value of your time by calling you and asking you to spend money." Securing the sale over the phone is a positive to this plan, but Frank would do better to consolidate his list of telephone calls to those customers who have a need for graduation flowers.

Erin decides to use a different technique. As with the other owners, she contacts customers instead of waiting for them to contact her, but she does it in a different way. Instead of making a telephone call asking for business, she only contacts a select group of customers who she knows have friends or family members who are graduating. She not only proactively contacts these customers, she does so in a way that will delight them while also reminding them that she is a great florist. Another important aspect of her marketing and sales strategy is the surprise flower delivery, which is the type of service customers are likely to spread to friends through word-of-mouth marketing. A customer who tells a few neighbors, "Erin's Flower Shop sent me a lovely bouquet the other day just because I am one of her customers," is the type of advertising that simply cannot be bought. This implies that Erin treats her customers exceptionally well. People might begin to wonder why their own florists do not send them unsolicited flower arrangements and might convince themselves that they deserve this type of treatment from a florist. Naturally, Erin will be their first choice when they need flower arrangements.

Notice that Erin's marketing and sales tactics take the most preparation. She needs to know her customers in order to know which of her clients need flowers during the graduation season. She also needs to know which of her clients will be most likely to buy additional flowers. Although Tina must spend time crafting the letters or coupons and Frank must spend time calling each customer, Erin's attempt at knowing her customers personally is the tactic that will pay off most.

It does take quite a bit of time and effort to get to know the needs of your customers. On the other hand, this is exactly the type of customer service to which an affluent customer will respond. Not only are you demonstrating that you have taken the time to get to know the customers' needs, you are also providing a valuable service by anticipating what the customers need before they are aware of it. You are also saving the customer time, and therefore, you save the customer money. Less time is spent seeking out a merchant to provide a service, and that time can be used for more productive tasks. So though you might not be offering a product or service at a reduced cost, you are still providing a savings. For many affluent customers, saving time is far more important than saving money when it comes to the purchase of goods and services.

CASE STUDY:
ADVICE FROM A
MARKETING EXPERT

Stephen Woessner
Marketing expert and author of
The Small Business Owner's Handbook
to Search Engine Optimization

In my experience, the affluent market cares about features, advantages, and benefits with the perspective of being able to turn that into specific dollars and return. For example, it is common to see a small-business owner say, "If you buy my product or service, we will save you more time, we will make you more efficient, and there is less risk in hiring us." Small-business owners need to figure out what any of that actually means.

As you position yourself for an affluent audience, you need to be more specific about the actual dollar value you can deliver. You must say something along the lines of, "Other clients who have hired us have experienced an increase in sales of 18 percent or more." When possible, give tangible, measurable numbers. Remove the ambiguity from the messaging. A great resource for this concept is Tony Parinello, who became popular for his VITO (Very Important Top Officer) books. He calls this process converting something to a hard or soft dollar value. It becomes more meaningful to affluent customers when you can tell them the hard or soft dollar value of the goods or services you will provide.

The importance of respect

You already know you have to display respect to your affluent customers whenever you deal with them, but you also need to treat your customers with respect when it comes to dealing with their private information. Suppose you have a database of affluent customers who regularly use your services. You worked hard to build up this database, and you are meticulous about ensuring that the information contained within the database is correct. You have the names of your affluent customers along with the names of their spouses and children. You have their contact information, including their postal addresses, telephone numbers, cell phone numbers, and e-mail addresses. You might have their birthdays, anniversaries, hobbies, pets' names, and other interesting information included in this database. Basically, you have everything you need to know about all of your affluent customers to provide them with the best in personalized service. It took you time and effort to create this database, and it is incredibly valuable to your business.

Now suppose another company contacts you and shows interest in this database. They want to have all the information you have compiled over the years about your customers, and though your first inclination is to say "no" to the request, the company counters your resistance with a generous offer to pay you handsomely for the information. It is difficult to say "no" to something that could make you so much money, and you also wonder if your customers would even realize you were the person who sold this information. What harm could it do?

Actually, the answer is that it could do quite a bit of harm, and for more than one reason. Think about the repercussions of selling off personal information you have compiled about your customers. You make your customers vulnerable to unscrupulous businesspeople who certainly might not have your customers' best interests in mind. These are the same customers you are supposed to genuinely care about, especially if you want there to be a professional relationship built on trust between you and your customers. You cannot claim to care about your customers on any level if you are willing to turn around and sell their personal information. It does not matter if this was information they provided you because they trusted you to keep it confidential, or if it information you compiled on your own from conversations you had with your customers and extra research you did. The fact that you are willing to pass this information along to the highest bidder does not say much about your professionalism and degree of care you have for your customers.

Damage the trust factor between you and your affluent customers and you destroy your credibility as a businessperson. Affluent customers can be incredibly secretive when it comes to personal details about their family — especially details about their young children — because they do not want to make themselves vulnerable to people trying to take advantage of them. If you do not think affluent people frequently encounter people who are trying to take advantage of them in one way or another, ask an affluent acquaintance to clear it up for you. There is a good chance your acquaintance can list several instances when he or she felt as though someone was trying to take advantage of them, whether in a financial way or otherwise. Many affluent customers are keenly aware when someone is attempting to take advantage of them, and they also assume trustworthy people will not attempt this.

In other words, your wealthy customers expect you to keep all business dealings with them to yourself. Just as you would not go around town telling everyone about an embarrassing incident an acquaintance of yours went through, you should not freely share information about your customers. Not only is it unethical, but it is a little sneaky if you are doing it for financial gain.

Some business owners assume if they do not promise to not sell customer information, then there is no reason why they should not do so if the price is right. Unless their customers specifically tell them to not provide personal information to other agencies, these business owners figure there is nothing wrong with doing so. It all comes down to whether you want your customers to truly be able to trust you. Anyone well versed in dealing with an affluent customer base knows that trust is difficult to gain yet amazingly beneficial when it is earned. Tossing that trust out the window by giving away personal information about your customers is a bad idea all around, even if you do not think they will figure out that you were the businessperson who sold the information. For all you know, the company you sell the information to might decide to use the existing relationship you have with your customers as a way to open conversation. Imagine your customers receiving a telephone call that starts out with, "Hi, we got your contact information from (your name), who said you would be really interested in hearing what we have to offer!" Even worse, what if the product this company offers is a scam? You just became a scam artist by association in the eyes of your customers.

Keep in mind that if you make statements about not selling personal information or sharing it with other agencies, yet you turn around and do so anyhow, you could be opening yourself up to legal action. Tell your affluent customers you will never sell their information or provide it to other agencies for marketing purposes, and stick by that pledge.

Selling and Marketing: A Symbiotic Relationship

Marketing will interest customers in your product or service, but your sales technique will seal the deal and result in a purchase. Use sales techniques designed specifically for this special group of customers. You cannot woo wealthy people with marketing designed for them and then deliver a less than stellar sales presentation. Do not promise an exceptional purchase experience if you are not prepared to deliver.

Your sales pitch

Sales pitches come in a wide variety of forms, depending largely on the product or service you offer. Your sales pitch to a room full of investors in a formal setting will be vastly different from your sales pitch to an individual customer who visits your jewelry store. Be prepared to offer a dazzling sales pitch at any time because you never know when a potential customer might present him or herself. Therefore, though you want to have a polished, rehearsed sales pitch available for formal presentations, you also need to be able to present the merits of your product or service in an informal setting. You might be surprised to find that plenty of business deals take place on the golf course or at a restaurant dinner table, rather than in the confines of a stuffy boardroom — particularly with the affluent.

Your sales pitch should not only tell your potential customer about how great your product is, it should also convey:

- What your product or service offers that the customer cannot get elsewhere. In other words, it should explain why your product or service is so special.

- Why the customer should come to you for a product or service instead of going to another merchant.

- How your product or service will enrich the life of the wealthy consumer.

These items certainly do not have to be presented in a bulleted list; in fact, you will quickly find that many affluent customers have little patience for stiff, forced sales pitches. An affluent customer wants the information presented in a way that allows him or her to make a decision quickly based on the facts presented. Therefore, you do not want to drone on about things that do not matter, and you also do not want to fill your sales pitch with fluff that does not offer any useful information. Bring to the table a nice mix of charm and personality married with vast knowledge of the product or service you offer.

Practice your sales pitch. Remember, you need to mingle among affluent people without feeling intimidated. Some salespeople have the ability to feel comfortable in nearly any situation, regardless of the position of the person they are speaking with, and this is a trait that can serve salespeople well as long as the confidence does not come across as excessively conceited or cocky. If you do not have the innate ability to appear comfortable in any sales situation, practice can be of great benefit.

Just as an actor rehearses his or her lines for a stage presentation, you should practice your sales pitch. Although it is preferable to practice your sales pitch with other people who are pretending to be clients, if you do not have any friends or colleagues willing to sit through your sales pitch, nothing is wrong with practicing in front of a mirror or while sitting in traffic.

Key points

It is not difficult to determine what information to include in your sales pitch as long as you know what environment the pitch will be delivered in and the expectations of the person or group you are pitching to. Pitching your product or service during a scheduled meeting in a boardroom will be far different than pitching spontaneously during a chance meeting at a social gathering. Just as you would not waltz into a planned meeting in a highly casual manner, you also would not whip out a PowerPoint presentation at a party in an attempt to pitch your product or service to a potential client.

Pay attention to how people react to you during a sales pitch, and be prepared to adjust your technique at a moment's notice. There is always a chance you might initially misread the tone and tempo of a potential customer or group of potential customers, so be ready to switch tactics if necessary. If your formal presentation seems to be falling flat with your audience, a less formal approach might grab their attention more effectively. Just make sure you do not make a drastic switch abruptly in a desperate attempt to gain control of the situation because this will simply appear chaotic.

Remember that affluent customers want to know why your product or service is something they should be interested in. Will it save them time or money? Is it something that they can only get from you? Is it something unique or highly coveted? When preparing the key points of your sales pitch, remember that your audience wants to know — in tangible terms, if possible — what the benefit of the purchase will be. If your product typically appreciates by 18 percent annually, include this information in your sales pitch. If your service has a track record of saving customers three hours each month, include this information, too. Tell your potential customers about the benefit of your product and service, and if the benefit is enticing enough, you will have piqued their interests.

If the product or service you sell does not necessarily have a tangible benefit, capitalize on what makes the product or service unique or special. Many affluent customers are motivated to purchase something when they think that they are buying something their neighbors do not already have. Suppose you are an artist trying to convince an affluent customer to buy one of your pieces. You have not yet built up a reputation as an artist, so you cannot necessarily make the claim that your art typically appreciates by a certain percentage. Although you can talk generally about how all art has the potential to appreciate in value, a better tactic for most affluent audiences is to talk about the amount of interest shown in your art. You could describe how you were profiled in an art magazine or received calls from overseas art collectors — but only if these things are true, of course. This shows the potential buyer that although you might not be a household name, you are on the cusp of exploding onto the art scene. This gives the wealthy person the opportunity to grab one of your art pieces before anyone else knows who you are, which becomes something the customer can brag about later when visitors comment on the piece of art. The customer will be able to say, "I purchased this piece of art before the artist made it big. I saw the talent before everyone else did."

Figure out what benefit you offer to your customers and then capitalize on that benefit when pitching your product or service. Your key points should not be made up of why you think your product or service is so wonderful, but rather why an affluent customer will think your product or service is so wonderful.

The elevator pitch

Not every sales pitch takes place with ample time to spare. Many affluent people are quite busy with convoluted schedules or simply do not have the desire or patience to sit through a full sales pitch before deciding whether to buy a product or service. This is why you need to perfect what is commonly referred to as an "elevator pitch." This sales pitch is a highly condensed presentation that should be easily understandable by most people and should be able to be presented within the amount of time it takes an elevator to go from the bottom floor of a building to the top floor. In other words, you should be able to convince someone to buy your product or services in a 30-second elevator ride.

For some salespeople, this is the main direction they take for pitching their goods or services because their service or product does not call for formal presentations. For example, a cleaning company that offers cleaning services to large office buildings might have to present a formal sales pitch to a room full of executives before a decision can made about whether to hire the cleaning company. However, a house cleaner who primarily works in affluent neighborhoods will likely have to master the art of presenting an elevator pitch. A homeowner is unlikely to demand a formal presentation from a potential house cleaner and instead will want a quick walk-through of the house and an immediate bid on the cost of recurring cleaning services.

Elevator pitches are shorter versions of a full sales pitch. Just as you should practice your full sales pitch until you can present it confidently, you should also rehearse your elevator pitch. Many people assume an elevator pitch is less stressful to prepare and present; however, a shortened sales pitch might actually be more stressful because the presenter is under pressure to present a great deal of information in a short amount of time while not appearing rushed. For many salespeople, this is a tall order. When your pitch is aimed at an affluent audience, it is even more important to make sure it is polished and concise. Your wealthy customer base is likely quite used to being on the receiving end of sales pitches, and if you falter in your presentation or try to present information that simply is not true, you will probably lose the chance to make the sale.

Body language

A good salesperson can read body language and knows when a customer is interested, disinterested, or downright annoyed — and adjusts the pitch accordingly. Your sales pitch is important, but the body language shared between you and your potential client can convey more than words. Affluent customers will respond well to salespeople who present confidence through body language, even if the customers do not consciously realize the salesperson's body language is presenting that air of confidence.

Your body language

Most of your body language is involuntary. You might not even realize you display nervousness or boredom while speaking to a potential client or delivering a sales pitch, but these and other emotions can be conveyed clearly if you do not know how to control your body language while dealing with customers.

Controlling your body language is not deceptive; rather, it is another tool you can use to communicate your message clearly while also putting your customers at ease. If you have ever been in a meeting where the facilitator was incredibly nervous, you probably noticed that it made all of the other attendees feel uncomfortable. As an additional bonus, if you learn to notice your own body language and control the image you are sending, you can also learn how to control your actual emotional response. If you realize you are showing certain signs of nervousness, you can take immediate steps to calm yourself and lessen the degree of nervousness.

While presenting a sales pitch, dealing directly in a sales transaction, or simply speaking to a potential customer, you want your body language to portray confidence and concern for the needs of the customer. Make sure your posture is straight and confident. Do not wring your hands together or cross your arms. These both convey nervousness or combativeness, depending on the context of the conversation. Keep your eyes centered on your client, and if you have a problem with maintaining direct eye contact because it makes you uncomfortable, focus your gaze instead to the spot in between the client's eyes. This will appear to the client as though you are looking directly into his or her eyes and will save you from having to keep a steady gaze.

About Your Customers

The body language you assume when speaking to an affluent customer might have to change if you are dealing with a client from another culture. For example, in some cultures, it is considered incredibly disrespectful to look someone directly in the eyes. Whether you market to an international or regional audience, there is a good chance you will encounter clients from a variety of cultures and should adjust your pitch accordingly. If you know you will soon be meeting with someone from a culture different from your own, make the effort to research the social expectations of that culture beforehand.

It might be worthwhile to have a conversation with the people close to you to find out what body language habits you exhibit. Many people are unaware that they absentmindedly twirl their fingers through their hair when talking with other people, pop their knuckles, or slump forward instead of sitting up straight. Ask your friends or family to pay attention the next time you are deep in conversation and tell you whether you have certain mannerisms you might not be aware of. You might be surprised to discover that the people close to you have already noticed such mannerisms but simply have not talked to you about them.

Nothing is wrong with displaying certain habits when hanging out with friends and family, but when speaking with affluent customers, body language needs to convey confidence and control. You will be hard pressed to find any customer — affluent or not — who is excited about buying products or services from someone who has body language indicative of nervousness or sheer confusion.

Try to keep your body language open. This means you should not cross your arms, cross your legs, or turn your body away from your affluent client. The message you want to portray with your open body language is this: "I am prepared to tell you the complete truth, and I have nothing to hide. Furthermore, I am completely receptive to whatever it is you want to ask me." Do not fidget, as this can be mistaken as an external sign of nervousness. Fidgeting includes tinkering with your pen or folders when there is no need for this movement.

Never answer your cell phone when in a conversation with an affluent customer. These customers are accustomed to being treated with utmost respect and attention, and if you answer a phone call, you shatter any hopes of conveying the idea that the customer has your undivided attention. No matter how politely you excuse yourself to answer the phone, this action will have a negative impact on the conversation.

CASE STUDY: ADVICE FROM A BUSINESS EXPERT

Todd C. Darnold, Ph.D.
Associate professor of organizational
behavior and human resource management
Creighton University

To my knowledge, there is little distinction between body language cues in the affluent and the nonaffluent; the differences we know of come from business studies of managers and people studying to become managers, so they tend to be more affluent-based on the sample. The general keys to body language concerning affluent customers are good solid handshakes with good eye contact. Engaged posturing is preferred by most, along with continued eye contact, engaging the person who you are in contact with, and leaning forward, which signals engagement versus leaning back and crossing ones' legs. The exception is when there is a connection between the two parties, in which case it often works well to mimic the posture of the other party to show you are of a similar personality. Body language signals comfort an interaction, as well as appear to act as a single personality. These actions send implicit signals to other parties in the communication.

In the study *Exploring the Handshake in Employment Interviews*, we found some interesting things that can easily pertain to body language and nonverbal communication with customers. For example, on average females had weaker handshakes, but when females did have firm handshakes, it had a huge positive impact. We also found that females can make up the gap between a weak handshake more so than males. It could be if they have a weak handshake, other cues would be taken into account to a greater degree than they would be for males. When females do have a firm handshake, they can especially benefit from assertive behavior in their body language more than males, whereas violating it can be harmful for a male.

When presenting sales pitches or dealing with customers within the United States, always being action-oriented, assertive, and adapting as the situation develops should be your starting point. Taking the time to learn how to react to people's cues is important. Although you do want to mimic body language, do not mimic odd movements, such as twitches and the sort, but do mimic the body positioning of the person you are attempting to impress. Be engaged if the person is engaged and relaxed if he or she is relaxed. You can use the other person's body language to change your approach based on their posture.

Abrupt changes in body posture are a signal that you have alienated a person for some reason. One of the keys is if you have empathy in the sense that you have an actual understanding of the person and you are taking cues from this person in the interaction. Anything you can do to get better at empathizing will make you a better salesperson and businessperson, particularly when dealing with an affluent customer base.

People who are affluent want to be engaged. If you are not making eye contact, they will find that problematic because they tend to be assertive individuals. These rules especially apply in a power-deficit situation; they will have an expectation that you are paying attention to them, and if you appear not to care, it will not go favorably for you in the end of the interaction.

Your customer's body language

Pay close attention to the way your client's body reacts to the things you say. If you can learn to decipher body language, you will be able to direct conversations away from topics that make the client uncomfortable and focus on the topics the client's body language indicates he or she is interested in.

You probably already know the signs of someone who is annoyed or distracted. The person will not look you in the eye and might focus more attention on a piece of lint on his or her pants, rather than on what you are saying. Before jumping to the conclusion that the person is not listening to you, however, consider cultural aspects. You should also consider that some people simply like to allow ideas to simmer before making decisions or replying to the things being said. Not all affluent people are adept at social graces either. Although the norm among affluent people is to be comfortable in social situations, some affluent people are simply not comfortable with people they do not know well. For this reason, before jumping to the conclusion that your client has already disregarded the things you are saying and decided to walk away from anything you propose, take a closer look.

Does your client verbally respond to you? If the customer stares out the window instead of looking you in the eye but does respond to the things being said in a natural, undistracted way, you might simply be dealing with someone who prefers to look out the window instead of looking someone in the eye. Reading body language is a delicate balance of noticing subtle nuances while using your gut instinct. Use the signs you get from both verbal and nonverbal cues to decide whether you need to change the subject or continue to pursue a particular topic.

Pay attention when body language changes dramatically. Suppose you are conversing with a customer who has come into your store and is eyeing an expensive rug. The client's body language initially indicates great interest in the rug. His eyes remain on the rug, he reaches out to touch the rug, and he talks excitedly about how the rug reminds him of his recent travels to Istanbul. When the conversation turns to the cost of the rug, however, he abruptly stops looking at the rug and looks you in the eye. His voice lowers as he repeats the price, and then he looks away. You can tell from his demeanor that he either was not expecting the price you stated or he routinely reacts to prices with an immediate introspection. It is up to you to decipher whether he actually will make the purchase or if he is talking himself out of the purchase.

What do you do in this situation? Always assume the customer has the financial means to make the purchase, no matter what the price of the product is. For this reason, the issue up for debate is not whether your customer can afford the rug but how you can assist your customer in making the transition from browser to buyer. You can first assume that the customer thinks his travels to Istanbul were interesting; otherwise, he would not have bothered to tell you about them. This is an excellent opportunity to bring the customer deeper into conversation with you, putting him at ease while also keeping him in your store instead of walking away from the purchase. It is also an excellent opportunity to use a technique used by psychotherapists called "mirroring."

Mirroring is the act of subtly imitating the body language of the customer. If he leans to the right, you subtly do the same. If he tilts his head to the side, you do the same thing. You do not want to mirror your customer in such a way that makes it obvious you are trying to mimic his body language. This is not a circus act; it is a method used in counseling to create an ease and camaraderie in a discussion between two or more people. Do not make it obvious that you are mirroring your customer's actions, but do take cues from the customer as to what body language is appropriate for the moment. A customer who leans in and whispers questions to you is not going to feel comfortable if your response is loud and from a far physical distance. Likewise, a customer who has a boisterous stance and speaks loudly is going to feel that your quiet, reserved responses are incongruent to the situation. Match the mood and body language of your customer if you want to create a relationship, even if that relationship only lasts as long as it takes to complete the sales transaction.

Trying to mirror your customer's body language will also make you more mindful of the body language used by your customer during the conversation. How many times does your affluent customer glance at his or her watch? Does your affluent customer immediately turn away from you when you approach and welcome him or her to your store? Does your customer run his or her fingers through his or her hair every time you try to finalize the purchase? These nonverbal cues can tell you it is time to switch tactics in an attempt to make the customer more comfortable in the situation, and ideally, with the purchase. Do not mirror quirky or nervous physical actions, not only because it will probably reveal your mirroring tactic but because it can make your customer feel examined or ridiculed. Do mirror subtle body movements, such as when the customer switches balance from one side to the other. You can also mirror your customer's voice inflexions. If your customer speaks excitedly and it is appropriate to be excited, mirror this speech. It shows that you understand your customer. Your client might not even notice that a camaraderie is being formed, but on a subconscious level, he or she might be more likely to decide that you can be trusted and are looking out for his or her best interests.

Why is it important to pay attention to the body language and verbal cues of your customers? Customers — especially affluent customers — might feel as though salespeople have no real interest in them and are only out to make as much money on their customers as possible. Consider what it is like for people who have worked hard to build their monetary worth only to find that most people work equally as hard to get them to spend it. It is no wonder that many affluent people approach all sales situations with an innate distrust. For this reason, if you hope to be successful in marketing and selling to affluent customers, you should be prepared to invest time and effort into getting these customers to feel as though they can trust you. Not only will it put them at ease, but it will also poise you to do business with them in the future.

About Your Customers

Do not make promises you cannot keep, and do not make claims about your product or service that are false. Perhaps you can make a sale to an affluent customer using deceptive methods, but that will be the only sale you ever make with him or her. And chances are good that your customer will not be shy about spreading the word about the deceptive sales tactics you used.

Some people are good at reading body language and other nonverbal cues; in fact, effective salespeople are typically great at reading body language in order to decide how to proceed in a conversation with a customer. Practice reading body language in everyday situations, such as while waiting in line at a movie theater or at the grocery store. Once you learn how to understand what people are saying without actually speaking, an entirely new category will open up to you with regards to knowing what your affluent customers are thinking when considering a purchase.

The following are some things to look for concerning body language:

- A customer who is conflicted about making a purchase might have one hand (or other body part) clenched and the other hand unclenched.

- A customer who does not feel comfortable with what he or she is about to say might cover his or her mouth before or while speaking. Another common nonverbal cue of discomfort with words is if the customer clears his or her throat in the middle of speaking.

- A quick darting away of the eyes while speaking might indicate that the speaker is not committed to what he or she is saying or is lying.

- A body stance that is open, with unfolded arms and wide-open eyes, is characteristic of a person who is receptive to the situation.

These are only a few of the things to look for when attempting to sell to an affluent customer, although you should always keep in mind individual differences and cultural considerations. Not all aspects of body language are universal. The way to decipher the body language of your recurring affluent customers is to actually take the time to get to know them; if you do this, you will quickly realize when a customer's body language is different from what it is usually like.

CASE STUDY: AFFLUENT CUSTOMERS IN OTHER CULTURES

Travis W. Vanderpool
International businessman

Many of my business dealings take place in China. I have noticed a huge difference in how business is conducted there as opposed to how business is done in the United States, particularly when dealing with affluent businesspeople.

Business people in China covet patience and honesty, so it can take several years before they adopt you into their business circuit. Even before that, if you are trying to conduct business, there is no such thing as a cold call. If I am trying to do business with someone in China, I have to find someone who has already done business with them in order to go see that particular company. You have to reach out to your educational or business network to find someone who knows someone within the company; everything is about reputation. It is about getting a personal endorsement. The person recommending you has to trust you will not ruin their reputation.

Having a meal with a potential business contact or customer is a huge sign of success within the Chinese culture. An important part of the meal is that the host will order for the entire table, and the host always orders more than enough food for everyone in attendance. If you finish all of the food on your plate, it is a bad reflection on the host because it signifies that the host did not provide enough food for everyone.

Typically, sometime after having a meal with a potential customer in China, you will be invited out to what is called business drinking. The whole goal of this is to get you drunk; what they want to do is to see how you behave when you are not in your right mind. There is a lot of toasting with a lot of protocol. The customer you are trying to engage will make a series of toasts; it is important to touch glasses lower than the host's as a sign of respect. Leaders will say *gan bie*, which means "bottoms up," and you have to finish the drink as a sign of respect.

Gift giving is also big; I always bring something as a sign of appreciation. Another important thing to know about conducting business in China is that the place of honor is always to the left. They are always lined up across from you, and only the senior leaders are the ones who do the talking and have prominent spots to sit. You can tell who the most affluent person in the room is because that person is in the place of honor.

Ninety-five percent of the population in China is rural, so as a businessperson, you are only typically dealing with educated people in big cities; their government regulates this by granting a permit to live in the city only to highly educated people. Not everyone can come and live in a big city like Shanghai. The people you encounter at business meetings within China will be affluent, with the focal point of your meeting being the one person who is most affluent. Everything is geared toward one person.

Who do you pitch to?

A family walks into your store and browses among some expensive items. Although your intention is to make all of the members of the family feel welcome, you have to quickly make the choice regarding which member of the family will get the highest level of attention. Many people make the immediate assumption that a salesperson's attention should go right to the family member who appears to be the head of the household. However, immediately turning your attention to whoever appears to be the main breadwinner in a family can be a faulty choice for more than one reason. For example, if you head straight to the father, you might insult the mother who can feel as though you made that choice simply based on the fact that the father is a man. On the other hand, turning your attention to the mother can upset her because she might feel that she has been typecast as the "shopper" in your mind simply because she is a female. Talk to the parents and the children might feel alienated, but talk to the children and the parents might feel as though you are trying to manipulate the children. What is the solution?

It is relatively safe to make some assumptions with affluent families. You can assume they have the money to spend on the purchase and that it might not be the breadwinner making all of the decisions. Although the breadwinner might make the ultimate decision, the spouse could also have a say. It might also be true that there is not one clear breadwinner between the two spouses, as both spouses might have high-paying jobs or be equal partners within a lucrative business. Whatever the financial situation between the members of the family, do not assume you know which member to direct your sales pitch to; if you get it wrong, you might offend or upset the person making the purchasing decision.

Instead, address the family as a whole and find out which member is actually there to do some shopping. Although there might be situations when each member has a purchase they want to make, often it is a matter of everyone coming along while one person makes a purchase. Maybe Dad wants a new set of golf clubs, or perhaps it is time to buy the daughter's first car. Whatever the situation, you can quickly find out who the purchase is for and who is in charge of giving the green light on the purchase; many times they are not the same people. This is particularly true when parents are buying a high-end item for a child; the child might make the final decision of what item he or she wants, but it is probably the parents who are actually going to open their wallets and pay for the purchase.

For this reason, you should initially address the entire family. If every family member feels as though you are on their side, the entire group will feel better about the purchase they make with you. Do not ever try to play family members against each other. For example, if parents have come in to buy a necklace for their daughter, do not pull the daughter aside and try to sway her toward a more expensive necklace than the one her parents have in mind for her. When selling, consider families to be a unified unit that needs to be courted from every angle. If you upset one member of the unit, you might lose the rest of the unit. Remember, affluent families are accustomed to salespeople desperately trying to get them to make purchases. If you try to play family members against each other, you will likely encounter a unified front from the family that will not result in your favor.

About Your Customers

The family scenario is merely one example of how important it is to understand who your customer is when you are attempting to sell a product or service. Take any assumptions you have about who runs affluent families and throw them out the window. Not all affluent families are led by middle-aged Caucasian men, and even families that do fit into this demographic might have a wife or child who ultimately makes the important purchasing decision.

In some instances, it will be quite easy to determine who is making the decisions. Suppose a couple walks into your showroom and the wife announces that her husband can pick out whatever he wants. This scenario reveals that while the wife might be the one to pick up the tab, the husband gets to make the final purchasing decision. However, always remember than when selling to the affluent, you need to court the group as a whole. Ignoring the wife and buddying up with the husband in this situation might turn out poorly.

Simply put, do not assume that the breadwinner within an affluent family will always be the one to make the final purchasing decision. Often, the breadwinner is a busy professional who must rely on his or her spouse to handle tasks such as making major purchases. Therefore, when a wealthy man's wife shows up in your office wanting to talk about hiring you to provide a service, you should never insinuate that she should call her husband to get the approval for the purchase. It is not uncommon for one member of a couple to work long hours and the other member to handle all the domestic affairs. Assuming that the person making the money is the one who needs to approve all the purchases is dangerous because there is a real potential to miss business by not taking the nonworking spouse seriously. Trust that if one spouse does indeed have to consult with the other spouse before making a final purchasing decision, this will likely be mentioned beforehand.

Chapter 6

The Successful Seller

You can spend a great deal of time attempting to profile affluent customers. What do they wear? Where do they vacation? How can they be spotted in a crowd? And although this information can be valuable, it is also important to have a look at the profile of a successful salesperson and, more important, the profile of salespeople who have experienced great success in selling to an affluent customer base. If you know what traits successful salespeople generally have, you can determine whether these are traits you have too — and if not, how you can get those traits.

Traits of Successful Sellers

Some traits are universal among successful salespeople, regardless of the customer base they serve. Successful sellers are personable, knowledgeable, enthusiastic, and believe in their products. This remains true whether the salesperson is selling cheap jewelry at a mass merchandise store or multimillion dollar diamond rings in an exclusive jewelry boutique. Differences abound when you look closer at the comparison between everyday salespeople and the salespeople who are selling to an affluent customer base.

Successful salespeople to the affluent have a knack for creating relationships with their customers. They pay attention to the things their customers say and remember when anniversaries and birthdays roll around. Customers feel as though the salesperson is an ambassador to a brand instead of simply a person taking their money. They feel as though the salesperson truly believes the product or service is worthy of attention. In other words, the salesperson does a great job of creating a positive impression with his or her affluent customer base, particularly when it comes to cultivating and maintaining relationships.

These salespeople are incredibly patient. When dealing with high-end items, these salespeople know affluent customers might need time to mull over a purchase. An effective salesperson knows that just because a customer does not buy the yacht or the summer home during the first consultation does not automatically mean that the sale has been lost. The salesperson will follow up with the client and ensure that the client gets exactly what he or she wants, even if this takes a little time.

Sellers who successfully deal with an affluent customer base are not as concerned with the volume of sales as traditional salespeople typically are. Although most salespeople measure their success in a day or quarter based on how many items or services they sold, salespeople who successfully deal with affluent customers look at the connections they made that day and consider these successes because they can lead to sales down the road. After all, a typical salesperson might sell 20 Hyundai vehicles in a month and consider this great success, but a salesperson who sells one Maybach in the span of a month has earned a considerably higher commission. Volume is not as important to a salesperson dealing with high-end items as it is to other salespeople.

Although it is important for any successful salesperson to have knowledge about the product or service he or she sells, a salesperson targeting affluent customers will have extensive — bordering on exhaustive — knowledge of the product. Any question posed by the affluent customer can be quickly and confidently answered by the salesperson, and a successful salesperson always stays up to date on the latest technological advances or updates with the product. The salesperson is not surprised by any question and is eager to share information about the product. The enthusiasm these salespeople have for the product or service they offer is infectious because they truly believe they are selling the best product.

Successful salespeople are not afraid to ask questions in an attempt to further clarify what an affluent customer needs or wants. Although some salespeople are too intimidated to ask questions because they are afraid it will convey that they are not knowledgeable, a salesperson catering to the affluent realizes that asking questions is an important tool in order to get customers exactly what they need. As long as the questions asked by salespeople are pertinent to the purchase and not based on a lack of knowledge about the product, most customers will appreciate the opportunity to clarify their needs.

These salespeople never make promises they cannot keep. Although successful salespeople cater to affluent customers in any way they can, they also have boundaries and do not allow customers to talk them down to prices so low that no commission can be made. These salespeople are savvy businesspeople in their own right, which only makes them better salespeople.

Salespeople who successfully sell to affluent customers are incredibly confident. They do not immediately allow their thoughts to turn to rejection when faced with a sales situation. Instead, they assume they will make the sale because they are confident in their own selling abilities and believe in the product or service they sell. Confidence also helps to put the customer at ease. Would you want to purchase a product or service from someone who appears timid or otherwise unsure of the product he or she is selling? Confidence not only makes salespeople more likeable to an affluent audience, it also portrays confidence in the product or service being sold.

Perhaps one of the most important traits of most successful salespeople who cater to affluent customers is that they do not lump all affluent people into one category. These salespeople do not disregard customers as nonaffluent based solely on appearance or demeanor. They treat all customers with the same respect they would treat customers who are already known to be quite wealthy, regardless of whether the salespeople know the customers are actually wealthy. You should treat all customers with respect, and anyone you employ to represent your brand should do the same. *You will learn more about selecting and training employees later in this chapter.*

Customers for life

Successful sellers understand that affluent customers will remember excellent customer service and will return to salespeople who make the purchasing experience enjoyable. For successful salespeople, the conclusion of a first purchase is not the conclusion to the relationship. Salespeople who excel at selling to an affluent audience will not only remember the customer and show delight when he or she returns, the salesperson will also maintain contact after the transaction is complete.

Suppose a salesperson successfully sells an expensive handbag to Mrs. Smith, a new customer. It is completely appropriate for the salesperson to send a handwritten note to Mrs. Smith when another new handbag design from the same designer is released, asking her if she would like to preorder the new handbag so that she can have it before anyone else in the neighborhood does.

About Your Customers

Affluent customers might expect more from their salespeople. You might be asked to do things that are out of the realm of your duties, but these are the extras that will set you apart from other salespeople. Instead of just selling an item, be willing to also wrap the item, deliver the item, or do any other reasonable thing the customer requests.

These salespeople become the go-to salesperson for affluent customers. The goal is to make your name synonymous with whatever it is you sell. When affluent customer Mr. Martinez buys his car from you, he is so impressed with the service and attention he receives that he automatically thinks of you every time the opportunity arises to purchase a new vehicle. When Mr. Martinez needs to replace his older car or needs to buy a car for his teenager, you do not want Mr. Martinez taking to the Internet in an effort to find the best deal on a new car. Instead, you want him to pick up the phone and call you, tell you what he is looking for, and then rely on you to get him exactly what he wants. His previous sales experience with you was so positive that he has no doubt you will deliver the car he wants with little effort on his part.

Of course, in the best case scenario, you will realize that Mr. Martinez needs a car even before he does. Perhaps he mentioned his teenager will be of legal driving age a year from now during the initial sales experience. Instead of simply hoping that Mr. Martinez will remember you when he is ready to purchase the car for his teenager, contact Mr. Martinez to ask whether he would like you to look for the perfect vehicle as the birthday approaches. Mr. Martinez has probably only just begun to think about purchasing the car, and with your one letter or telephone call, you have relieved him of what could prove to be a tedious process. Remember, even if you are not necessarily saving a customer money, saving time is certainly a motivator for most people. Not only do you save Mr. Martinez time, but you also make it clear that you were listening during the initial sales experience and that you are looking out for his best interests. This is an excellent way to retain customers and a common trait of salespeople who successfully sell to wealthy customers.

A repeat customer is one less customer you have to go out and court for new sales. In most cases, it takes far less effort to retain an existing customer than it does to find new customers. If it is your hope to successfully sell to affluent customers, always keep in mind that your efforts should go beyond the initial sales experience because you want these customers to return to you for additional purchases. You also want to eventually get to the point in your sales career when you have such a large affluent customer base that you spend more time dealing with your existing customers than you do with trying to get new customers to buy from you.

The beginning of a career

Salespeople who wind up with an affluent customer base rarely do so out of luck or chance. These are salespeople who are willing to work hard, know the ins and outs of the product or service they sell, and have the confidence to deal directly with people who can be incredibly intimidating. Selling to affluent customers is more than a simple sales job; it is a career that can be lucrative if correctly done.

If your career as a salesperson to the affluent is in its beginning stages, you will find that the saying "patience is a virtue" is something you will have to remind yourself repeatedly of. It might take time for you to build a potential customer's trust, let alone build the trust of an entire base of customers. The eventual result of all your hard work will certainly be worth it if correctly done, but it can take time before you establish yourself as a reputable and successful salesperson with wealthy customers.

Selling you

When you are involved in a sales transaction with affluent customers, you are not only selling the product or service but also the idea that you are a salesperson who is likable and can be trusted. Affluent customers can afford to deal with whichever salespeople they want and expect a level of service that is simply not found at average retail stores.

Consider the difference between the purchase experience average consumers have when buying a camera and the buying experience an affluent customer can enjoy. Average customers visit whichever retailer they prefer or looks for sales beforehand, and after they arrive at the store, they have little choice about which salesperson they deal with and have no control over the interruptions that occur. Salespeople might have to take a phone call or ask you to wait while they attend to another customer, and salespeople in average stores do not have time available to truly cater to customers at an excellent level because their quotas are likely based on volume sold rather than customer satisfaction. Customers who are pleased with the transaction are more likely to return to that particular store, but they are unlikely to ask for the same salesperson every time they want to make a purchase.

Now examine the purchasing experience of an affluent customer shopping for a camera. Affluent customers might immediately find salespeople they have worked with in the past and ask to see a few cameras. The affluent customer expects that the cameras selected by a salesperson will be suitable, but more important, an affluent customer also expects the salesperson will be knowledgeable while also making the transaction pleasant. Affluent customers will not contact a salesperson whom they have had bad experiences with because affluent customers have the luxury of picking and choosing whom they do business with. A salesperson who is rude, unknowledgeable, or simply does not do well in social situations will probably not do well selling to the affluent, no matter what product or service the salesperson is selling.

If it sounds like a tall order to become a successful seller to affluent customers, it is probably because it certainly can be. It helps if you have a natural knack for dealing with people and have a charismatic personality, but there is much more to it than that. You have to know your product inside and out, and you must be willing to do whatever it takes to make your customers happy. Is it worth it? Most successful salespeople with an affluent customer base say that the effort is certainly worth it. Successful salespeople working on commission boast impressive incomes, and business owners selling directly to affluent people find their businesses thrive as a result of their successful efforts to market to this particular demographic. Getting started in selling to the affluent can be a slow and seemingly tedious process, but the payoff can be tremendous.

Capitalizing on who you are

In order to exude the confidence needed in order to appeal to an affluent customer base, you need to take a close look at who you are and what you bring to the table. First, do not dwell on any negative aspects of yourself. Instead, focus on your positive attributes. The key is to get yourself to a point where you have the confidence to stand tall next to important people who might otherwise intimidate you. You cannot be an effective salesperson to the affluent if you get anxious every time a high-profile person walks into your store. Your anxiety might come across loud and clear to your customers, who might in turn interpret this as an inability on your part to competently serve them.

About Your Customers

Dress the part when presenting yourself as a premier salesperson. This means your clothing is stylish and in good repair, your hair is groomed, your shoes are free from scuffs, and your nails are not ragged or chewed. You will have a better chance of getting affluent customers to relate to you if you mirror your appearance to theirs.

How do you turn nervousness into confidence? Although you might find that the more you deal with affluent customers the more comfortable you become, the goal is to spend as little time in the nervousness phase of your career as possible and quickly evolve into a salesperson who is not only at ease with any customer, but who can also make the customers feel at ease with making a purchase. You can start this process by convincing yourself you are not nervous and that you are at ease in any sales situation. If you have never tried to convince yourself of anything, you will find that it is not a complicated process and is something that is most effective when done repeatedly.

Anytime a thought enters your mind that compels your nervousness forward, such as "I am so nervous" or "There is no way I am going to make this sale today," immediately replace the negative thought with something positive. Imagine a cheerleading squad in your mind saying, "I am not nervous!" or "I am in control of this situation!" or "The client wants to buy something and will buy it from me!" Although these statements might seem overly optimistic, the great thing about this type of internal positive talk is that it can quickly calm your nerves and will eventually become the default thought your brain turns to when facing a sales situation. Instead of walking into a sales situation with an affluent customer with negative thoughts of inevitable failure floating through your mind, you will walk into sales situations feeling confident and relaxed. This will translate into an ease that makes you more appealing as a salesperson, particularly among affluent customers who expect to receive the best customer service available.

Capitalize on your strengths. If you have a great smile, be sure to flash your smile whenever dealing with affluent customers. If you have a knack for calming people down, use your ability to bring calmness to a purchase situation that might otherwise be stressful, such as during the purchase of a home. If you have an ability to bring levity to situations, do so when appropriate. The trick is to figure out what makes you a great salesperson and then to use these strengths. Affluent people are generally accustomed to dealing with people who are sure of themselves and good at what they do, and for this reason you need to be prepared to put your best foot forward.

You should keep in mind that you might have weaknesses as well as strengths, and although you cannot completely disregard these weaknesses and assume you will never be able to improve upon them, you should keep in mind that putting your best foot forward sometimes means not leading with your weaknesses. If you have problems with making small talk, do not push small talk. Instead try to direct the conversation toward the product or service you are selling in as polite and conversational way as possible. If you force yourself to talk about the weather when you know it will sound strained and ridiculous, you will make the sales situation awkward. Awkward situations rarely result in sales to affluent customers because they want to feel at ease and comfortable; after all, this is what they are used to when dealing with salespeople.

Do not simply accept any weaknesses or shortcomings you have as a salesperson. Recognize what your weaknesses are and work toward improving them while keeping in mind that no one has the ability to master every single sales situation. Use your strengths to your advantage and work on your weaknesses as best as you can, but if there are some aspects of your personality that you simply cannot change — or fake —make up for your shortcomings with the positive attributes of your personality.

You are your own brand. In other words, if you combine yourself with the product or service you offer along with the reputation for the company you work for or own, you have one big package to offer to affluent customers. As a salesperson, do what you can to accentuate your brand, and because you are one aspect of the brand as a whole, focus on making yourself the best salesperson you can be.

Your Employees

You are not the only person representing your product or service. Everyone who works on your behalf — whether it is the salesperson who deals with customers face to face or the receptionist who answers your phone — should have the same understanding of the importance of customer service as you do. Imagine what it would be like for an affluent customer to enjoy an impeccable buying experience from beginning to end but then to have that positive image of the company shattered when the delivery person arrives at the front door speaking rudely and wearing a stained shirt smelling of cigarettes. All it takes is one negative experience to taint a customer's perception of a company.

Stress the importance of excellent customer service, no matter what role the employee has within the structure of your company. If your employees will spend a great deal of time dealing directly with your customers, provide comprehensive training that empowers these employees to present confident and knowledgeable demeanors to all customers. Make it clear to every one of your employees that less-than excellent customer service is unacceptable and will simply not be tolerated. Along those same lines, be sure to reward those employees who do provide the type of customer service you want your company to provide. Be liberal with your verbal praise when an employee gives customers an excellent buying experience, and if possible, offer rewards in addition to commission, bonuses, or paid time off.

It is not enough to simply assume your employees know how to deal with affluent customers. Even if your employees come directly from another business that caters to a wealthy customer base, they might not come equipped with the right skills needed for the product you offer. If you are in the process of opening a new business, you have the advantage of training your employees from the beginning to ensure they provide customer service that is up to your expectations. If you obtain an existing business or if you have already been in business for some time, it might be time to review the way your employees deal with customers.

It might not be your employees' fault if they do not provide impeccable customer service. They might provide adequate — yet not excellent — customer service because that is all they have been exposed to and do not understand the importance of providing outstanding customer service to an affluent customer base. In these instances, it is the business owner's fault for not specifying what actually constitutes excellent customer service. Not everyone understands the fundamentals of dealing with customers in such a way that the customers come away from the experience feeling as though they enjoyed the purchasing process. It is ultimately the responsibility of the business owner to make sure all employees understand what is expected of them.

If you are not sure where to start when it comes to setting guidelines for your employees, start with making sure your employees understand the distinction between affluent customers and other customers. Although all customers should be treated with a great deal of respect, affluent customers are incredibly vital to the health of the business. These are the customers who can afford to make purchases today instead of tomorrow and who can bring in additional affluent customers if they are impressed with the product or service they purchase. You do not want to teach your employees to try to figure out who is affluent and treat everyone else with subpar service, but you do want to make sure your employees understand there is a definite reason why affluent customers are to be treated as well as possible.

Consider offering a commission program to your employees if you do not do so already. You will probably find salespeople are willing to go that extra mile when their own income is riding on a sale. One option is to give salespeople a percentage based on the sale amount or to give a flat rate commission per sale. Another option is to set a quota for the expected number or amount of sales you expect salespeople to make, and then if they reach that goal, they earn a bonus. Many business owners find the best option is to offer commission on a percentage of the amount of the product or service sold. If a salesperson knows every single opportunity to make a sale is also an opportunity to make a profit right in that moment, he or she might try harder to provide the customer service necessary in order to wow the customer. Furthermore, salespeople might be more aggressive in finding opportunities to up-sell if they know the monetary amount of the sale will correlate with the amount of their paychecks.

Giving a commission that is not based on each individual sale but is instead based on a number of units sold can actually backfire, according to Salary.com. If salespeople are more concerned with selling units as opposed to striving for a high monetary amount, there is a good chance that these salespeople will steer customers toward buying multiple items that do not cost as much instead of trying to compel the customers to buy single items that cost more. It is difficult to blame the salespeople in a scenario like this because, after all, they are simply trying to do what they can in order to earn the highest commission. For this reason, take a close look at your commission program and make sure you are rewarding excellent customer service, as well as compensating salespeople when they make a sale instead of turning the act of selling into some sort of numbers game that encourages salespeople to sell whatever they can to whoever walks through the door. Salespeople need to gauge the needs of the customer instead of simply seeing dollar signs.

If you do not have employees working under you because you are a one-person operation, consider bringing employees on as your business grows. If you are successful in selling to affluent customers, there is a good chance you will soon find you cannot handle everything on your own. If you are an excellent salesperson, the employee you bring on might not be meant to replace you as salesperson but instead to handle administrative tasks that would otherwise keep you from having face time with your customers. Whatever task your employees take on, be sure to convey the idea that you expect every single interaction with customers to be handled in a respectful and attentive way. You decide if you allow employees second chances when it comes to dealing with customers, but when dealing with affluent customers, one single bad experience with a rude or inattentive employee can cause significant problems for your business. In other words, if an employee simply is not providing the type of customer service you know your wealthy customers need, it might be time to invite that employee to be successful elsewhere.

Finding the right employees

Why is it so important to find the right employees to join your team? No matter what capacity your employees will work in for your company, and regardless of whether they will encounter your affluent customers on a daily basis, your employees are one part of what makes up your brand. You want your brand to be superior in all ways, and staffing your company with excellent people is one way to work toward that goal.

It is not enough to scan a prospective employee's résumé and decide based solely on that information whether someone will make a good salesperson or representative. First, think about what the role of the person will be within your company, and then set up a face-to-face interview based on who made the best impression on paper. Even if someone has a stellar résumé that seems to indicate he or she is a perfect fit for what you are looking for, this might not always be the case. Even a telephone interview might not be enough to tell you if someone is right for the job.

About Your Customers

Using an employment service can be a great way to find applicants who have been prescreened as having had experience dealing with affluent customers.

Ideally, you should look for employees who have experience in dealing with affluent customers. People who have already worked with this special consumer population might know how to successfully cater to affluent customers, but you cannot count on experience alone to be the reason why you hire someone. After all, just because a person once worked in an environment that involved dealing with affluent customers, it does not necessarily mean this person was good at what he or she did. So although it is a good idea to look for employees who do have this type of experience, you do not want to use this as the single qualifying factor for employment with your company.

Pay close attention to the first impression you get when meeting an applicant for a face-to-face interview because this will tell you much about what the first impression customers will get from this person. Does the applicant appear at ease and friendly? This is a good sign that the applicant can take a stressful event, such as an employment interview, and still turn it into something pleasant. Does the applicant seem incredibly casual, laughing at inappropriate times and not seeming to pay attention? This behavior can also indicate nervousness, so think about how this type of person would do when dealing with affluent people. Do you want your salespeople or other employees to seem casual and blasé? This is not the attitude that affluent customers will generally respond well to. Your employees should appear confident and respectful while also conveying a level of expertise or knowledge that puts customers at ease. If the applicants you interview do not convey these traits, do not hire them.

Take a look at how an applicant is dressed along with how well he or she is groomed. You do not necessarily need your employees to show up to the interview wearing the most expensive business suits available and dripping in expensive jewelry, but your applicants should at least look as though they take pride in their appearance. Even inexpensive clothes can look impressive and expensive if they are well cared for. When you look at your potential employee's overall appearance, pay attention to the initial impression his or her appearance gives you. If your first thought is that the employee probably does not know how to work a clothing iron, let alone a brush, then this is probably not the ideal candidate for you.

Remember that your employees are an extension of you and are an indication to customers of what image your company is trying to convey. It might take more time and effort to find the right employees who can deliver exactly what you are looking for, but when you are dealing with an affluent customer base, this extra time and effort is absolutely worth it.

Chapter 7

The Ten Commandments of Attracting and Keeping the Wealthy Customer

> *"Consumers are statistics. Customers are people."*
>
> Stanley Marcus, former Neiman Marcus CEO

T o be successful, you not only have to put your concentration toward attracting affluent customers, but you also have to put a great deal of effort toward keeping these customers. You want to be the first person who comes to mind when your customers start thinking about a purchase they want to make. Provide the best product or service combined with the best buying experience and there is an excellent chance that your customers will return to you time and again.

Never fall into the trap of thinking that you need to focus all your attention on getting new customers. Instead, complement your efforts of getting new customers with cultivating relationships with the customers you already have. If you provided a great experience at a reasonable cost for what you were offering, retaining your customers should not be incredibly difficult. Follow the "Ten Commandments of Attracting and Keeping the Wealthy Customer" to make sure you have a steady stream of new customers coming in while also compelling your existing customers to return to you.

First Commandment: Respect the Customer

Respect should be present in every interaction you have with your customer. Even if you start to form a friendship with the customer, do not allow this to dissuade you from being consistently respectful. As long as the customer is buying your product or service, the position of power belongs to the customer, and this is something you should not forget.

Remember that most affluent customers expect a high level of customer service, no matter if it is the floor salesperson they are dealing with or if they are having a face-to-face meeting with the CEO of a company. It is possible to be polite yet not respectful, and this is a horrible combination because it appears condescending to the customer. It can be a delicate balance of being respectful while also attempting to appear approachable and — if appropriate — casual. The simple solution is to consider every customer worthy of your respect and to act accordingly. Frankly, a salesperson who has issues with showing respect to all customers will have issues with being successful when dealing with affluent people. It will be difficult to influence a wealthy customer to open his or her wallet if the customer does not feel as though there is a level of respect being provided by the salesperson.

Show respect by always delivering what you promise. If you disregard the deadlines set to provide goods or services, you are basically conveying a message that you do not respect the customer or his or her needs. Telling Ms. Hanson that you will have the product to her on Tuesday, and then allowing Tuesday to pass with no product delivered and no explanation provided will probably be perceived by Ms. Hanson as a blatant insult. There is little chance you will receive return business from Ms. Hanson in the future as a result. Affluent customers have the choice to go with a different merchant or service provider for future purchases, even if that means an increased cost, so when you are dealing with wealthy people, it is incredibly important to do everything you can to not drive them away. It is far too easy for these customers to move on to someone else.

Another aspect of ensuring you treat these customers with respect is making the effort to have face-to-face meetings with them. If Mr. Martinez wants to talk to you about catering for his event, set a time to meet with him in person instead of suggesting you call him over the phone — or worse yet — send him a form letter and checklist to fill out via e-mail. Respecting your customers means making the transaction as simple as possible for them, so if that means setting time aside to meet face to face and maybe add a little more to your workload, so be it. Mr. Martinez will remember the ease of the transaction and return to you in the future.

Second Commandment: Listen to the Customer

What should be going through your mind when dealing with an affluent customer? For unsuccessful salespeople, their minds are swimming with calculations of the potential commission they will earn from this customer, or perhaps even they think about the game tomorrow or about how they would rather be anywhere else than standing there helping out a customer. If you do not provide affluent customers with your full attention, not only will you probably be ill equipped to help them adequately, but there is also a good chance the customer will notice he or she does not have your undivided attention and might decide against buying anything from you.

Really listen to what your customers are saying. Mr. Mathis tells you he is looking for a new television for his game room and then goes into a story about how he visited a neighbor and loved the surround sound in the game room. If you are truly listening, you can easily conclude that Mr. Mathis is looking for more than a simple television; he is actually looking for an entire theater set-up for his game room. He might not even realize this is what he wants, so it is your job as a salesperson to help him figure it out. A big difference between average customers and affluent custom-ers is that while they might both not know exactly what it is that they want, it is the affluent customers who have the ability to not balk at the solution if it is expensive. Mr. Mathis wants his game room to have the same entertainment package as his neighbor's, and if it costs more than he thought it would, he will probably still pay for it simply because it is what he wants.

There is more to listening to your customer than exactly what he or she says to you. Listen for what is not being said, as well. Just because a customer does not say she is willing to pay an exorbi-tant amount of money for the landscaping on her home does not mean she is unwilling to do so. Ask questions until everything is clear. How do you know when everything is clear? It is when you have an understanding of what the customer wants without having to ask any further questions, and the customer appears at ease with the solution you have presented. When in doubt, ask questions. Most affluent customers would greatly prefer to answer questions instead of having the salesperson guess and then wind up with something that is not really what the cus-

anted. Keep in mind that sometimes customers will not

clear idea of what they want either. If the customer's request seems vague, it is your job to sift through whatever details
the customer can provide and get enough clarification to present
the perfect product or service. Putting it into the perspective of
the customer actually needing your help might help; you are not
simply a salesperson. You are a solution provider.

Third Commandment: Stay Close to the Customer

This is especially important if you want to retain affluent customers. You need to learn the story of each of your customers
in order to form a personal connection while also anticipating
future needs. You should know the personal preferences of your
customers, and not only in respect to the types of things they like
to spend their money on. Perhaps some of your customers like to
sip on coffee while going over a contract with you, but Ms. Cru-
soe does not drink coffee and would much rather have an iced
tea when meeting with you to go over contracts. The next time
she walks into a meeting with you, there is a pitcher of iced tea
waiting for her on the table. She is immediately impressed and
flattered that you would remember her preference, and this also
puts her at ease when dealing with you.

Know what your customers do for a living, and if they own their
own businesses, know what their businesses do. This can help
you anticipate their needs. It is not necessary to plan a full-blown

investigation regarding your customers' employment or business, but it makes sense to have some knowledge about what they do and what their needs are. The same goes for the details regarding their lifestyles. You will remember from earlier chapters that not all affluent people prefer to live a flashy lifestyle. Suppose Mr. Andrews is one of those people. He is quite wealthy but does not like to broadcast his financial status to the world. When he walks into your jewelry boutique to purchase something for his wife, you will not start with the biggest, gaudiest diamond ring you have in stock. This move would demonstrate to Mr. Andrews that you have not been paying attention in earlier transactions with him and might make him uncomfortable dealing with you.

Use the knowledge you gain in every transaction you have with the customer. If you know that a particular customer has Pomeranians at home, ask how the dogs are doing when this customer visits with you. A simple "How are Bobo and Fluffy doing?" will work well, or you can try something along the lines of, "I saw some beautiful Pomeranians in the park the other day and could not help but think of Bobo and Fluffy." The point is to make the customer feel at ease while also making the transaction more personal. If your customers feel comfortable walking into your store or office because they know they will feel like they are chatting with a friend instead of going through an aggressive sales pitch, it is more likely that your customers will return to you in the future.

An important aspect of forming a personal relationship with your affluent customers is recognizing that you might be exposed to privileged communication. Consider a situation where a customer casually mentions to you that his company is on the verge of introducing a new vending concept to the local area but is still in the process of finding an appropriate manufacturer. He does not tell you that this is confidential information because he figures that there is no reason you would tell anyone else about this new plan. What would happen if you then shared this information with a friend in a crowded coffeehouse, and your customer's main competitor just so happened to be sitting in a booth nearby and overheard your conversation? Or, worse yet, what if you posted on a social networking websites that you are excited about the new vending concept that your customer's company will be bringing to the area? You might think there is no harm to things like this, but business information being leaked before the company is ready to release the information can be a huge problem. This does not pertain solely to business information; your customer might reveal things about his or her personal life or the lives of his friends or business associates, and this should all be held in the strictest confidence. The information you are privy to should stay under lock and key, no matter how juicy or interesting it might be.

Fourth Commandment: Anticipate the Needs of the Customer

If you have already formed a good rapport with your customers, you should be in a good position to anticipate their needs. Suppose that Mrs. Connor has come to you for the last two years on the same date asking for a beautiful bouquet to be delivered to her mother's grave. Instead of simply waiting for Mrs. Connor to visit your shop to request the bouquet, contact her beforehand and ask if she would like you to prepare the bouquet. Not only will she be impressed that you remembered the date, but it will also be one less thing she will have to stress over.

Being proactive and offering your goods and services when you think it might be appropriate can increase your business quite a bit. In some instances, such as with the instance of Mrs. Connor, it might be that your customer has not yet decided whether he or she is going to make a purchase, or your customer might not be set on which merchant or service provider to seek assistance from. By anticipating the needs of the customer, the problem is solved and you get business that might have otherwise gone to your competition if you had not been proactive.

Maybe anticipating the needs of wealthy people seems like a foreign concept to you and you are not quite sure how to go about doing so. If this is the case, try putting yourself into your customers' shoes. If you were the customer, what would you need?

What recurring needs would you have, and what might you not even realize you need or want? Although it is true you can never truly know everything about your customers, using this trick to visualize what needs your customers might have can be an important exercise.

An important note should be mentioned here. Although it is great to anticipate the needs of your customers, it is incredibly important to not cross the line into being presumptuous with your customers. For example, using the example of Mrs. Connor's flower bouquet, you would not go forward and create the bouquet and then send it to her mother's grave all without first consulting with Mrs. Connor. Imagine if she had decided against sending a bouquet or had already ordered the bouquet with another florist, and the next thing she knows she is looking at an invoice for the bouquet you sent without first checking in with her. There is a good chance you will have an angry customer on your hands. She will not pay for the bouquet, she will not use your services in the future, and furthermore, she will probably tell her friends about the whole incident. Anticipate your customer's needs, but do not presume that your customers will be happy if you make decisions before consulting with them first.

Allow your customers to help you anticipate their needs. In the case of Mrs. Connor, it would have been quite easy to simply ask her if she would like to make the bouquet an annual order. Stress that you would be honored to have the responsibility and would be happy to handle it personally every year. This is a far better plan than just assuming that Mrs. Connor would have this need every year and would want you to fill the order.

Fifth Commandment: Make the Customer Feel Important

You already know to treat your customers with respect, but making them feel important takes this a step further. When you are dealing with a customer, either face to face or over the phone, you need to make sure you convey the message that your customer is your number one priority at that moment in time. Your cell phone should not ring, your attention should not be diverted, and you should treat your customer in a way that signifies it is your extreme pleasure to be in a situation to provide assistance.

This can be a difficult task, especially if your position has you running in several directions at once. The best salespeople can make customers feel as though everything else has been abruptly dropped because they walked into the room. You want your customers to feel as though their presence is an important event. It should feel as though you saw the customer and immediately though to yourself, "Stop everything! My most important customer just walked through the door!"

This does not mean that you gush over a customer's purchase as though he or she just solved the world hunger crisis, but it does mean to make sure the customer realizes that you consider his or her business important and that you are grateful he or she chose to do business with you. When your customers call you on the telephone, do not put them on hold. When they send you e-mail, reply promptly. When your customer asks you a question, get the answer. This is the type of customer service that makes a lasting impression on the people you want to make a lasting impression on.

It can be an interesting balancing act. There might be times when you have so many things going on at once that it seems like an impossible task to stop what you are doing and attend to your customer. Remember, if you are unwilling or unable to make your customers feel important, plenty of other merchants and service providers out there are happy to do so. Without your customers, you have no business. Keep this in the mind the next time you have the opportunity to assist one of them.

Sixth Commandment: Know the Power of Passion

Have you ever had a conversation with someone who is incredibly passionate about the topic at hand? A person's passion can be infectious, even if you did not start the conversation with any sort of interest in the topic. A person who is excited about something can make other people excited too, and this is why you can leave a conversation convinced you should give skydiving a try, even if you never had an interest in this activity before speaking to the avid skydiver.

You need to be passionate about the product or service you offer. Not only is this important in the sense that you will feel more rewarded from your work when you believe in the product or service you offer, but your passion will be noticeable when you speak to potential and existing customers. If you are incredibly excited about what you are offering, people might also be more inclined to be interested.

Conveying a positive attitude will do wonders. Do not treat your customers as your therapists by telling them all about your family problems, health problems, or frustrations from the day. No matter how close you might feel, you are inevitably going to lose some customers if you start allowing your sales interactions to become opportunities to tell them all about how crummy your day has been. Also — and this should go without saying — you should never talk about how your customers have money and you do not, even if you present in a joking way. Comments like "Hey, if I had the type of money you have, I would definitely buy this product," only promotes a distance between you and your customer. Some affluent people are uncomfortable with their wealth being pointed out because they know many people in the world are not nearly as privileged as they are. Your goal is to make the sales experience as pleasant and comfortable as possible, and pointing out the vast financial gap between you and your customers will probably make your customers incredibly uncomfortable.

Speak highly of yourself and your product, but keep the emphasis on the product. It is true that you want to convey the image of someone who is confident, but the ultimate goal is to convince your customers that your product or service is amazing. Never glaze over the product or service you offer because you want to spend more time talking about you.

Part of being confident in yourself and your product is having the courage to disagree with a customer, though this has to be done in the most respectful way possible. Remember that affluent customers do not simply want a salesperson who will nod and smile no matter what; they want a solution to their needs. Suppose your specialty is fine wines and a customer comes into your shop looking for a certain wine. After speaking to the customer and finding out the menu that will be served with the wine, it is obvious to you that a different wine would far better complement the meal than the wine the customer is looking for. Because of the confidence that stems from your expert knowledge of your product, you should feel comfortable suggesting an alternate wine. Your suggestion should sound more along the lines of, "May I suggest a red wine to complement your meal? It will truly bring out the subtleties of the flavor," as opposed to "You really need red wine if you are going to serve beef. To serve anything else would be an atrocity." Although some salespeople might be nervous about offering alternatives because they wonder if the customer will see this as an offhanded insult, particularly when the customer seems quite confident in his or her needs or wants, confident salespeople know the customer will appreciate a respectful suggestion. The key to offering an alternative to a customer is to do so in a confident way without even a hint of condescension.

Demonstrate that you are an out-of-the-box thinker. You have an excellent opportunity to increase your sales by taking what your customer wants and adding to it to make it even more spectacular. It is important to periodically review the product or service you offer and figure out ways to augment what you already offer.

Seventh Commandment: Over-Deliver on Customer Service

People who market and sell a product or service know that customers respond positively to excellent customer service, but it is important to remember that providing beyond-excellent customer service is the way to stand out among your competition when providing services and products to affluent customers. You want to give your customers a reason to come back to you, and if you exceed their expectations with the customer service you provide there is a good chance you will be who they think of when the time comes to make another purchase. The majority of the affluent customers you deal with are more than willing to spend a little more for excellent customer service.

Of course, this does not mean your sole concern should be providing customer service that wows your customers because this is simply one aspect of the total package you should provide. Combine your amazing customer service with an outstanding product or service. Offer a complete package for the needs of your customers. You want them to be confident that they will receive exactly what they are looking for from you and that they will enjoy the best customer service available when they deal with you.

What does over-delivering on customer service look like? You already know to anticipate the needs of your customers and to offer suggestions, but there is more to it than that. Look for anything that can save your customer time, as this is one of the keys to providing the best customer service to affluent customers. Every sales scenario provides the opportunity to over-deliver on your customer service. Consider an example where a customer brings a bicycle into your specialty bike shop for repair. Instead of telling the customer when the bike can be picked back up, offer to deliver the bike to your customer's front door when the repairs have been completed, and furthermore, make sure to specify that you will be happy to come out to pick up the bike for any future repair needs because you understand how important your customer's time is. Provide customer service like this, and there is an excellent chance that when the time comes for this wealthy customer to buy a high-end bicycle, you will be the first one the customer thinks of.

Not every customer wants to be fawned over, so it is important to read your customer's body language and listen carefully to what is being said. You never know if a customer — no matter how affluent — might feel incredibly uncomfortable with a salesperson eagerly offering to make a home delivery, even though this is not a generally offered service. If your customer appears uneasy about any of your offerings, do not feel compelled to push the matter. You certainly do not want to annoy your customers or make them feel uneasy about dealing with you, so if you offer a special service in an attempt to over-deliver on your customer service and your customer does not appear interested at all, do not insist. It is one thing to eagerly offer a special service, but it is another thing entirely to eagerly and persistently offer a service that has already been declined. Do not forget to watch your customer's body language and do not assume that your customer declining the service is simply a result of your customer trying to be polite and really wanting the service after all.

Eighth Commandment: Keep Your Promises

One of the quickest ways to anger a customer is to make promises you cannot (or do not intend) to keep. This wrecks your credibility and makes it unlikely that customers will return. You might also find that customers take a broken promise as a fundamental insult. Customers have to put trust into a merchant or service provider, so if you promise to have a product in your customer's hands by a certain date or a service completed at a certain time, the customer will assume this promise will be fulfilled. If the promise is not kept, the customer might feel as though he or she has been swindled. Simply put, do not make promises you cannot keep.

Some salespeople feel nervous about telling customers they are unable to provide a product or service by the time set by the customer, but it is far better to be realistic in your estimates instead of making promises you might not keep. You might be tempted to say yes to anything and then work your hardest at making it happen, but what do you do when you cannot deliver on your promise? Suppose you promise to complete a landscaping project for a wealthy customer's backyard within a month, knowing full well that similar projects have taken you at least three months in the past. You agree to the unrealistic timetable because you really want to work in the neighborhood because it is full of wealthy people who might hire you later for more landscape work. You convince yourself that you will be able to get the project done, but then three weeks later when it becomes obvious you will not meet the deadline for the project's completion, you must ask the customer for more time. You then find out that the customer needed the project finished in a month's time because he was going to host a charity gala in his backyard, and he is understandably furious that his backyard will not be ready for his important event. In this instance, your intention of earning a solid reputation within an affluent neighborhood has backfired; your customer will have to publicly cancel or move his event, and when the people invited ask why the event had to be changed, you can be sure that your customer will be vocal about your broken promise.

Think beyond reputation when considering how important it is to keep your promises to your customers. You can face legal action from customers if you do not deliver on your promises, and remember that affluent customers have the money to hire lawyers to aggressively pursue the matter in court, if necessary. Obviously, making promises you cannot keep to your customers can be a costly mistake. Maintain your credibility by keeping the promises you make, and if something out of your power occurs to make it impossible for you to keep your promises, keep in contact with your customers and do something to make everything right.

Ninth Commandment: Revere the Testimonial

Your marketing should not rely solely on the testimonials provided to you by your past and existing customers, but these should nonetheless be considered quite valuable. You will place testimonials on some marketing materials or might display some testimonials in your place of business, but the point is to convey that other customers have tried your product or services and have come away satisfied. Testimonials can come in a variety of forms; you might have satisfied customers send you letters thanking you for your assistance, or you might receive short notes on your Facebook page that say your customers are happy. No matter how your testimonials are received, consider them golden. You should also receive permission from your customers before using any of the testimonials for advertising purposes, particularly if you provide sensitive products or services (such as a mortuary, medical service, financial service, etc.). Customers might take offense to having a personal letter written to you distributed to a wide audience.

Whenever you receive a testimonial, thank the customer profusely and ask permission to use the testimonial in your marketing efforts. Most customers will have no problem with this, and many customers expect this is what will happen if they submit a testimonial. Some customers will ask that their last names are not used or that initials are used instead of their names. Especially honor these wishes because you want to make sure these customers come back to you again for your product or service. It is also important to make sure you do not edit or revise the testimonials in an attempt to make them sound better than they originally did. It is one thing to correct misspellings or to edit for brevity, but if you take a genuine testimonial and revise it into something you wish it would have said yet still attribute the original writer's name to it and refer to it as a genuine testimonial, you are setting yourself up for problems.

Imagine if you wrote this: "Thank you for your prompt response to my plumbing problem. Your technician was very nice and professional. I will use your services again in the future."

Now imagine if a testimonial with your name on it showed up in a marketing campaign from the same plumbing company and said this: "No other plumbing company has ever been as prompt as your company! I was blown away by how nice and professional your technician was. From now on, your plumbing company is the only company I will ever use because I know I will get the best service and the friendliest technicians!"

The second testimonial is an obvious embellishment from the first and has been shaped and formed into what the business owner wishes the customer had really said in the first place. Switching the customer's words around is not only unethical, it sends a message to the customer that the first testimonial just was not good enough. What are the odds that this customer will ever call this plumbing company again after something like this happens? It is not likely that taking an original testimonial and switching it around will help foster trust in a customer. Affluent customers are generally not as quick to allow their names to be put on something like a testimonial as average customers will be, so when you do receive a testimonial, resist the urge to embellish. The customer's name on any testimonial might be enough of an endorsement in itself.

How do you compel affluent customers to write a testimonial for your business? The key is to make sure your customers know how much you would appreciate the testimonial. This does not mean a simple sign near your register that says, "We appreciate your testimonials!" Instead, consider asking customers who have expressed their gratitude for your services to compose a testimonial. Stress that their testimonial will be especially important and appreciated. You want to convey the idea that this testimonial is of monumental importance because it comes from one of your most important customers. If your company has an online presence, make sure customers can submit comments electronically; it is easier for some satisfied customers to send off a quick e-mail thanking a company for a job well done as opposed to sitting down and composing a letter written by hand. You want to make it as easy as possible for your satisfied customers to express gratitude.

If your business offers a product or service that generally results in a "before and after" photo opportunity, ask for permission to take photographs before you provide the product or service and then again afterward. Testimonials from satisfied customers are great, especially when they come from highly respected affluent customers, but a tangible example of great work coming from a set of before-and-after photos might compel prospective customers to pick up the telephone.

Testimonials can take some work to get, but they are worth the effort. It is true that affluent customers generally tend to socialize with other affluent people, so a testimonial from one customer might reach other customers who might consider it a personal recommendation if they run in the same social circles.

Tenth Commandment: Never Let Them See You Sweat

Be relentlessly confident in the product or service you offer, and be relentlessly confident in your own abilities. Affluent people can be incredibly intimidating, especially if you do not have much experience dealing with successful, wealthy people. Whether your customers earned their money by clawing their way up the corporate ladder or if they were simply born affluent as a result of generational wealth, these customers can be intimidating simply based on their station in life. Even if they are quite cordial and humble, unintentional intimidation can be present.

Counter this intimidation (real or perceived) with solid confidence on your part. Although you do not want to appear cocky in your dealings with affluent customers, you certainly do not want to appear as though you are not sure of yourself. Remember that most affluent customers are accustomed to dealing with colleagues who are just as confident as they are, so they will feel more at ease dealing with you if you are sure of yourself.

Stand up straight, look customers in the eye (when culturally appropriate), speak confidently, and do not allow intimidation to dissuade you from putting your best foot forward. Affluent customers want to deal with people who know what they are talking about and can deliver the product or service exactly as the customer wants. Even if you know your product or service backward and forward, and even if you can deliver exactly what the customer is looking for, if your demeanor conveys nervousness or uncertainty, customers might decide against going to you for your services. They want to deal with product and service providers who convey the message that the job will get done, and furthermore, it will get done in the best way possible.

It can be difficult for some people to portray an overt sense of confidence, especially if they are not confident to begin with. Remember that body language has a huge part in this, but being confident in your ability to deliver what you promise also has a lot to do with the overall image you portray. *See Chapter 5 for a refresher on body language.* Keep your accomplishments in mind when speaking to potential customers, and use self-talk to help bolster your own confidence. Self-talk can include phrases such as "I am the best jeweler around," or "I can give my customers exactly what they are looking for," or even "I am about to dazzle these people with what I can offer them." Run these phrases through your mind before dealing with the customers who intimidate you. Your confidence level will soar, and this will make you more appealing to customers who expect to always deal with the best of the best.

This is certainly not to say that there will never be times when you feel overwhelmed. There will be days when you feel incredibly weighed down with work and would like nothing better than to let everyone know you simply cannot handle your workload. Instead of allowing your customers to see you sweating as a result of your nerves (and perhaps making your customers nervous as a result), present a calm and in-control demeanor at all times when interacting with current and prospective customers. The same goes for when you find yourself in public places, especially if you offer products or services locally. You do not want to walk into a coffee shop and loudly complain to your friend about how you will never get all of your work done or how your customers demand too much because you never know who might be listening.

CASE STUDY: AFFLUENT CUSTOMERS ARE DIFFERENT

Jason Heitbrink
Area director
N2 Publishing

One piece of advice is to not treat affluent customers any differently than anyone else, in the sense that you do not want to walk into a situation with a wealthy customer with an "I am not worthy" attitude. Rather, you have to have the belief that you are on a level playing field. You do need to let them talk more because they are used to having their ideas valued. These customers respect people who have self-confidence. You don't give them all the control, but you give them enough for them to feel they have control. Make suggestions in a manner that lets them feel they are making decisions while you are leading them toward a decision.

How you deal with these customers also will depend on your product. What is the problem you solve, and how does your business solve it better than anyone else? You have to create a need for your service and make them want to have what their neighbors have in their homes. If you are going to give a deal, it has to motivate the customer to want the deal. Saving time is huge for wealthy customers versus a small savings on price.

In my experience, it seems like a larger percentage of affluent customers react more to little issues than other customers. You have to listen to what they are saying and then offer prompt solutions to their problem. They expect a certain level of service you would not necessarily give to your other customers and expect resolution either for free or expediently. There is less of a go-with-the-flow mentality, and they have high expectations. If they make enough of a ruckus, they know they will get what they want. Not all affluent customers are the same, though. The other extreme from the entitlement mentality is the humble affluent customer who is more understanding and who has reasonable expectations toward a solution.

Chapter 8

Dealing with Difficult Affluent Customers

> *"Dealing with people is probably the biggest problem you face, especially if you are in business. Yes, and that is also true if you are a housewife, architect, or engineer."*
>
> Dale Carnegie, author and lecturer

I t does not matter if you offer the top-of-the-line product or offer a discount bin of clearance products; you will run into customers who are incredibly difficult to deal with. Whether they make demands that simply cannot be met or if they are downright rude, you should equip yourself to deal with these customers so that when the moment occurs, you are not surprised and you know how to react.

Demanding versus Rude

If you are not accustomed to dealing with wealthy customers, it might come as a surprise how demanding this population can be at times. In most cases, it is not a matter of the customers being rude, but rather it is simply a product of these customers being used to getting exactly what they want when they want it. Because many affluent people are in high-power positions with regards to their occupations, the demanding personality they display when purchasing goods or services is merely indicative of the way they behave in most business transactions. This demanding personality works to their advantage in business, so it is not a shock that they would appear demanding when dealing with other businesspeople or salespeople.

Demanding customers who are wealthy also might have experienced situations in the past where a demanding demeanor got them what they wanted with another merchant. This behavior has a track record of being successful, so why not use it again? These customers are also accustomed to getting whatever it is they demand because other merchants have wisely bent over backward in an attempt to keep them happy.

Do not take an affluent customer's demanding personality as a personal insult. Instead, regard it as a product of the customer's needs, and then do what you have to do to meet those needs.

If you tell a customer a product will take two weeks to receive, and the customer responds with, "That is not going to work for me; I need it in a week," this is not the customer being rude. It is an opportunity for you to prove you are the type of person who can get things done and who additionally understands that your customers have needs that must be met. Demanding people can sometimes come across as being arrogant and rude — in fact, some of them are indeed arrogant and rude — but as long as the customer does not blatantly insult you, use the incident as an opportunity to dazzle the customer. If you can indeed get the product to the customer in a week, do so. If not, apologize profusely and offer alternative solutions.

Insulting Behavior

Not all customers have learned the fine art of dealing with other people in a cordial way, though it can generally be said that people who reach a certain level of affluence have learned to deal with people quite well. It is difficult to run a company, lead a charity, or do anything that involves managing other people successfully without having some sort of people skills.

Problems arise when you come into contact with affluent customers who either do not have the skill to be cordial to everyone or who look down upon anyone else who is not wealthy. Although these people are the minority of this group (most affluent people are quite nice and do not treat people poorly), if your main goal is to market and sell to affluent people, you are bound to encounter people like this. This can be especially perplexing because it has been drilled into your mind that word of mouth is everything, so the last thing you want to do is to react negatively to a wealthy customer's behavior for fear that the customer will then turn around and tell the rest of the community about your unprofessional behavior.

Relax, and realize that the minority of affluent people out there who are jerks are well-known as being jerks among their peers. If a person who is incredibly hard to please and who typically treats people poorly tries to spread the word that you were rude in a business transaction, most people will roll their eyes and wonder who the real jerk was in that scenario. This does not give you carte blanche to fling insults at rude customers, of course, but take solace in the fact that you cannot please everyone.

About Your Customers

Monitor your posture when dealing with an irate customer. If you stand with clenched fists or with a puffed-out chest, you will only make the situation tenser.

You have a choice when dealing with a rude affluent customer. You can bite the bullet and continue serving the customer in whatever way he or she needs, and then when the transaction is complete, you can no longer pursue a professional relationship with that customer. You can indeed choose to not serve the customer at all, but do this at your own risk, as mentioned above.

On the other hand, you might simply decide that putting up with the customer's rudeness is a small price to pay for the profit you will bring in after the completion of the transaction. If this is the route you choose, you should be the person to deal with this particular customer, even if you have a staff of employees you could unleash. You have the ability to see past the rudeness and look to the eventual dollar signs, but your employees might not have that capability. Just remember that if you accept rude behavior from a customer — affluent or not — there is a good chance that this customer will assume this behavior is acceptable for all future dealings with you. It is up to you whether this is something you are prepared to accept.

Listen, Then Fix

Affluent customers can get particularly vocal when they feel as though a merchant has somehow wronged them. Maybe you did not deliver a product in time or perhaps you did not respond to a telephone call in a timely manner, but whatever the cause of the customer's anger, it is important to listen to what the customer has to say, apologize for the issue, and then find a resolution.

You might not feel as though you are actually in the wrong, but that is not necessarily what is important when dealing with wealthy customers. They want to be heard, and they want you to have the same level of concern over the issue as they have. So if this means spending half an hour on the telephone with an affluent customer who was upset that your store was closed on Thanksgiving Day, go ahead and spend that half hour on the phone listening. Tell the customer you understand the frustration and can see how being closed on Thanksgiving might be a big inconvenience for customers. Assure the customer that you will reevaluate the practice of closing the store for holidays, and thank the customer for bringing all of this to your attention. Apologize wholeheartedly for having inconvenienced the customer.

You might think that all of this will have to be said through gritted teeth because you cannot imagine someone would have the nerve to complain about closing a store so employees could spend time with their families on a holiday, but keep in mind the way you would deal with the problem: You should not agree that closing the store was wrong but instead convey the idea that you understand the frustration. You should not say you promise to keep the store open on holidays from now on but instead assure the customer you will reevaluate the policy. Even if that reevaluation means you decide that yes, you will be closed on holidays, you did indeed conduct the reevaluation nonetheless. Thanking the customer might seem ridiculous, but what you actually are doing is thanking the customer for being so passionate about the service or product that you provide. Lastly, you are not apologizing for closing the store but instead apologizing for having inconvenienced the customer. This is the key to dealing with complaints from affluent customers; really listen to what they are saying, make sure the customer knows you are listening, and then suggest resolutions to the problem.

When you are in the wrong

Chances are good that, once in a while, your customers will come up with valid complaints, whether it is a product breaking or a service not being provided as specified in an original contract. When this is the case, there is no dancing around the verbiage you use to appease clients. You need to listen to the problem, apologize wholeheartedly, and then make it right.

If a client comes to you with a valid problem, it is not the time to jump on the defensive and try to find a way to make it the customer's fault. If you (or your employees) did not deliver what you promised you would deliver, you are in the wrong and you need to fix the problem. If you can do this in a swift and urgent way, there is a good chance you can salvage the relationship you have with the customer who brought the complaint to your attention. If you fix everything well enough, there is a good chance you might improve the image your customer has of you. See mistakes as opportunities to learn and to demonstrate how you can fix problems in an impressive manner. For example, if you were contracted to create the perfect birthday party for your client's young child, but the person you hired to be the clown at the party does not show up, you better be willing to jump right into the clown suit yourself in order to deliver on your promise.

Ongoing customers

Always keep in mind that there are not nearly as many affluent customers as there are customers in other financial demographics. This means that if you manage to catch the attention of affluent customers, it is in your best interest to keep their attention so that they will return to you for business in the future. Marketing is not just about initially grabbing people's attention; it is also about keeping their attention. Affluent customers might be more demanding and might require more attention, but the extra effort you will be required to put forth is worth it for the benefit of your future revenues.

Chapter 9

Marketing and Selling is Ongoing

"Every advertisement should be thought of as a contribution to the complex symbol which is the brand image."

David Ogilvy, "The Father of Advertising"

W hen most people think of marketing, they think of a single advertisement or other singular instance of a method used to familiarize people with a product or service, which hopefully elicits a desire to purchase the item being advertised. Along those same lines, when most people think of the act of selling, they think of a moment when a salesperson is directly in front of a potential customer, trying to compel a sale. Although these examples are snapshots of what marketing and selling are about, they merely scratch the surface when it comes to marketing and selling to affluent customers. With this special group of customers, marketing and selling are both ongoing processes. This is because you want to grab the attention of affluent customers and keep it as opposed to making a single sale and then turning your attention to the next customer who walks through the door. Affluent customers can be quite loyal to brands they like, so your goal should be to become the brand these customers like.

Ongoing Marketing

Marketing to affluent customers can be quite different from marketing to other customers for a variety of reasons, but one of the most important things to remember is that the marketing should never stop when dealing with these customers. Even if there is little chance of a sale, staying in contact with existing customers is a tactic that can prove to be quite valuable. The goal is to stay on these customers' minds, so when the time comes to make a purchase, they naturally turn to you for their needs.

For this reason, set money aside in your marketing budget for special promotions that are designed to do nothing more than remind your existing customers of what great service they receive from you. Here are a few examples:

- An interior designer does the decorating gratis for a new women's shelter and places banners all over the shelter announcing the decorating was done for free. The interior designer does this because the board of the new shelter is populated by many of the same affluent customers the interior designer either already has an existing relationship with or would like to someday work for. He or she also knows when people provide generous donations — such as free interior decorating without asking for a big pat on the back — the members of the board make sure these people are appropriately recognized, so he or she will get her advertising without asking for it. This conveys to the affluent board members that this is the type of interior designer who is a good person, and this might be the first person they think of when the time comes to commission interior decorating for their own homes or offices.

- A professional calligrapher sends handwritten notes to all existing customers on their birthdays and anniversaries. Although the calligrapher knows this will not necessarily result in an immediate response from customers who need calligraphy services for invitations and other things, it keeps the calligrapher in these customers' minds while also conveying a personal relationship between him or her and the customers. Personal notes like these can be quite powerful when trying to establish a relationship with customers, especially considering the increasing rarity of handwritten notes appearing in people's mailboxes nowadays.

- A high-end jewelry store offers free jewelry cleaning services to existing customers, as well as anyone else who would like to use the cleaning service. Although it does take time and resources to do the cleanings, the owner of the jewelry store knows that offering this valuable service (and doing it well) gets customers to think of that particular jewelry store when they want their jewelry pieces to get a thorough cleaning. The jewelry store might even offer a pickup and delivery service to existing customers for this cleaning service. Although this might seem to contradict the ultimate goal of getting customers to step into the store to have a look at the inventory, remember that affluent customers are different. Often, these customers do not necessarily have to browse display cases before knowing what they want. A personal delivery of a cleaned jewelry piece by the owner of the shop might evolve into an impromptu conversation about a particular jewelry piece the customer wants to purchase, and of course, which the owner will be happy to promptly deliver.

- A restaurant hosts monthly dinners to invited guests where the food is free and the guests are able to sample the menu items offered by the restaurant. The invited guests are chosen from the affluent neighborhoods in the community and are treated to the best selections offered by the restaurant. The dinner takes place in a private room, and the invited guests are not expected to pay for the food they eat or their drinks and are not even expected to tip the servers. Although giving away free food might seem like a bad idea when solely concentrating on the profit for that particular evening, bringing affluent customers into the restaurant and treating them to a wonderful experience might bring in customers who might not have stopped into the restaurant otherwise. These are the customers who will return if they like the food, who will book the private room for parties, and who will want to have large events catered. These are also the customers who will talk to their friends about the experience and make it sound like something special. When Mr. Jones tells Mr. Smith that the restaurant was delightful and the food was delicious, this will be filed in Mr. Smith's brain, so the next time his wife wants to go out to eat, Mr. Smith says, "Mr. Jones told me about this great restaurant. Let's go there tonight."

Marketing does not have to mean a billboard or a website, though these can be successful ways to reach your customers depending on your situation. It is incredibly important to think outside the box when trying to think of ways to market to affluent customers. Find ways to make an impression on customers to where they have a positive response to your product or service, and your chances of being successful increase exponentially.

Do not allow your out-of-the-box marketing efforts to backfire. The interior designer who offers free services to a charitable organization but then does a bad job or falls far behind in the schedule is not making a good impression on the people he or she is trying to impress. The professional calligrapher who sends personalized notes out to customers but ends up sending sloppy notes or sends them on the wrong date is actually doing more harm than good for his or her business. The jeweler who provides free jewelry cleaning but then does a poor job with the cleaning or actually loses pieces in the delivery process is promoting distrust among customers. The restaurant that hosts affluent customers for free once a month but that does not provide good food, has rude staff, or worse yet, gives everyone food poisoning is only working toward an earlier closing date because of the bad reputation this restaurant will get.

Whatever you do for marketing efforts, do them excellently. Remember that whatever you present to potential or existing customers — whether they pay for it or not — is a reflection of your business. Think of it this way: if you walk into a bakery and are offered a free cookie to sample, and that cookie is so disgusting you have to spit it back out, you are not going to think to yourself, "Well, that must have been a bad cookie because it was free, so let me buy a dozen cookies to see what those are like." Free or not, this cookie is a reflection of the bakery as a whole. Any marketing effort you present to your potential or existing customers should be a true reflection of the amazing product or service you offer, period.

Ongoing Selling

As previously mentioned, if you get to know your customers well enough, you will begin to realize what their needs are and be able to respond to those needs before your customers even know the need exists. An aspect of this is understanding what your customers' needs are and responding by figuring out ways to meet those needs, even if this is outside of the realm of your business's typical dealings. Suppose you own a boat dealership and notice that some of the customers who come in to browse talk about how they would love to own a boat, but they do not know the first thing about driving a boat — or, for that matter, even maintaining a boat — so they wind up walking out without having made a purchase. Instead of giving vague recommendations to these potential customers along the lines of, "Oh, it is not so hard; you can pick it up in no time," or even something like "I can give you a list of people who teach how to handle boats," think about meeting the need as part of the sale.

Perhaps the customer would be much more comfortable if you as the owner of the boat dealership offered to personally teach customers how to handle a boat out on a lake. Take it a step further by offering a free year-long maintenance plan with a boat purchase, which takes the tedious task of maintaining the boat out of the hands of the customer. By offering these options to your customers, you have done a few things:

- You have made them feel important. Why else would the owner of a boat dealership be willing to take time out of his or her busy schedule to teach a customer how to handle a boat? The customer assumes the owner must think highly of him or her in order to make an offer like this. If it is a standard offer, you do not have to mention it unless the customer asks.

- You have removed the obstacles for the sale. The price of the boat is not the issue stopping the customer from making the purchase, but the time investment is. Remove the obstacle, and this greatly reduces the reasoning for not buying the boat.

- You are selling an experience. Instead of just selling a boat, you are selling the experience of owning a boat without the hassle of trying to figure everything out without guidance. It is far easier for a customer to envision sailing the seven seas if he or she knows that lessons will come from someone who knows a great deal about boats.

What if you do not personally want to offer services like this, no matter how affluent your customers are? Prepare to lose out on some sales, or find someone to add to your staff who can hold a special title (such as master boating instructor or something similar) and take the reins for these tasks.

Selling more

You and any salespeople who work on your behalf should be well versed in the act of the upsell, which means compelling a customer to buy more than he or she originally intended to buy. A customer comes into your store intending to buy a laptop, but your salesperson is able to talk the customer into buying a higher-end laptop than the customer originally wanted and also compels the customer to purchase some additional software, a service plan, and a customized laptop bag to go along with the new computer. Maybe the salesperson talks the customer into buying new laptops for his family of five, along with the additional software and other products to go along with them. Salespeople need to remember that affluent customers can generally afford to buy more than what they have expressed interest in, and as long as the additional purchase makes sense, they might easily be talked into buying more.

That is an important distinction: the additional purchase has to make sense. Many affluent customers already feel as though they have a huge target on them when they walk into a sales situation because it might be obvious they can afford to buy expensive items. This is why it is important for salespeople to never convey the feeling they are suggesting the additional purchases simply because the customer has money. Instead, the salesperson should make a genuine attempt to find out what the customer wants or needs and respond accordingly with appropriate suggestions. This is also where it is incredibly important to make note of what the additional products or services customers are looking for and to offer these. Make every affluent customer who walks through your door feel as though his or her needs have been met and problems have been solved by the time the transaction is completed.

When dealing with affluent customers, there should be no "standard" sales pitch every single customer has to endure when trying to make a purchase. Instead, salespeople need to listen to find out what would best suit the customer's needs and ensure those needs are met.

Recipe for Sales Success

If your salespeople do not know how to deal with affluent customers, it is your duty to teach them if you want your business to be successful.

- Teach your salespeople to truly listen to what the customer says. Salespeople should hear more than, "I want to buy a laptop." If that is all they hear, they are going to see dollar signs and start pushing the customer toward the most expensive laptop before actually finding out what the customer needs in a laptop.

- Teach your salespeople to ask the right questions. Questions such as "How much do you want to spend?" can backfire. Instead, ask questions that indicate a desire to fulfill the customer's needs and find the perfect product. This includes questions such as "What will you use the laptop for?" or "Are there specific features you are looking for in your laptop?"

- Teach your salespeople to be patient and spend time with affluent customers. Imagine that an affluent customer walks into your computer store and asks one of your salespeople to show him or her laptops, to which the salesperson responds with a wave toward the laptops and offers no further assistance. The customer does pick out a laptop, and then the salesperson starts trying to up-sell by offering additional products. The problem is that this salesperson did not earn the right to upsell, at least not in the affluent customer's eyes. If your salespeople are not willing to give attention to your customers, you are eventually going to run out of customers.

- Teach your salespeople to be the authority when it comes to the product or service they offer. A salesperson who can speak authoritatively on a product or service will appear trustworthy and can offer educated suggestions for additional purchases. Discourage your salespeople from presenting an authoritative front if they do not understand the product or service. If they are asked questions they do not know the answers to and then start making things up to try to appear authoritative, your business will lose credibility. Remember that your reputation as a business is incredibly important when dealing with affluent customers, so do not allow salespeople to wreck that reputation.

If your business offers an excellent purchasing experience, your customers will remember this and are more likely to return for future purchases. Buying a product or service from you should never be difficult or unpleasant. If affluent customers know that every time they deal with you (or your salespeople) they will have their needs met in a pleasant way, they are more likely not only to return to you in the future, but also to recommend you to other people.

Ensuring that every sales experience is pleasant and solves the customer's problem or need sets you up for future success. There are not many companies that can make the claim that their customers always enjoy the purchase experience, but if you can make that claim, you will find that affluent customers will return to you time and again. You will also earn a solid reputation that helps your business grow. Always keep in mind that every single purchase experience is an opportunity for future growth. You simply cannot know if a customer running into your store to buy a cheap cord is the same customer who will be so impressed by the way the sales transaction went that he or she later returns to your store to purchase several computers for her office. Do not look at your customers as one-time customers whom you should try to milk as much money out of as possible before they walk out of your store. Instead, regard each customer as someone who can be a lifelong customer and figure out what you can do to ensure that this happens. The more effort you can put into a single instance of a customer transaction, the better your customer will regard your service and might return in the future for additional purchases. One of the best things about dealing with an affluent customer base is that these are the customers who might return for something quite expensive, so your goal should be to make a lasting impression during the sales experience.

Always Marketing and Always Selling

Your reputation as a professional is ongoing and is not only confined to the instances when you are acting on behalf of your business. Look for other opportunities to present yourself to affluent customers in a positive light, even if you are not actively attempting to sell anything at the time. It is important to remember that when it comes to affluent customers, business often takes place in social settings as opposed to in a boardroom or within the confines of a shop. If you can find a way to make yourself present in these social situations, you increase your chances of making future sales.

Consider the example of organizations such as the Rotary Club, the Shriners, alumni groups, and professional associations. These groups form a camaraderie among the members because of the common affiliation they all have. Suppose an affluent customer decides to renovate his or her kitchen, which is no small task because the kitchen is huge. Instead of flipping through the phone directory or searching online, the customer immediately thinks of you because he or she has met you several times at networking meetings for a community organization and remembers your company renovates kitchens. The customer does not need to go through the arduous task of finding a suitable kitchen renovation company because he or she feels as though you can trusted because you have always presented yourself in a friendly and professional manner.

Communities also offer you the opportunity to serve in a position of power in the form of an elected position or volunteer role. Affluent people are typically in positions of power, so this not only gives you the opportunity to meet affluent people but also gives a commonality between you and your affluent customers. Although you might have no interest in running for a city council chair or going through the process of trying to get elected as mayor of your town, you should look into other opportunities to serve in a position of power. Volunteer for scholarship committees, agree to help judge a local competition, join the leadership board of your church, or get involved in other ways that present you to the public in a position of power. It is not just about getting your name out there; you want to convey the idea that you are similar to your affluent customers because you have a certain degree of power. Even if the roles you take do not necessarily give you any real degree of power, it is the perception of power that makes you more appealing to wealthy people.

Chapter 10

Troubleshooting Your Marketing Efforts

"It was a wealthy family, and they heard me talk about movies, and they told me I should go into movies. That's the benefit of hanging out with rich people; they have no sense of what is or isn't possible."

Michael Patrick Jann, actor and director

Affluent customers offer something average customers generally do not offer; they can buy things that would make some people cringe because of the sheer cost, and they generally offer loyalty to merchants who offer them the best experience. Getting your product or service widely accepted among affluent customers might also result in a trickle-down effect when people who are not necessarily affluent will figure out a way to also get their hands on what you offer, whether it is a matter of them shifting their budgets or whipping out a credit card. If you can make your product or service seem like something affiliated with wealth, you open up new doors among customers you might not even be targeting. Even if you target your marketing efforts solely to a wealthy customer base, do not be surprised if this actually winds up expanding your average customer base in the long run.

Keep Going

Affluent customers can be a tough target market. Although there are certainly ample statistics and research to tell you what affluent customers prefer and what their spending habits generally are, you probably will have a difficult time succeeding in selling to these customers if you presume every single affluent customer will react to you in the same way. Human behavior can be predicted to a certain extent, but there is no way for you to accurately predict what products or services will appeal to affluent customers in every single scenario and for every single customer.

This is why it is so important to pay special attention to your customers' behavior and to the things they say when interacting with you. What excites them? What makes them appear uncomfortable? What products or services do they talk about? Every interaction with an affluent customer is an opportunity to learn more about this particular group's behavior. Catalogue these interactions in your mind to help you predict future behavior, but make sure you always keep in mind that not every affluent customer can be lumped into the same behavior pool as the others.

About Your Customers

Practice makes perfect, especially when dealing with affluent customers. Insert yourself into situations where you can watch their behavior and learn from it.

The more you deal with affluent customers, the easier it will become to figure out what your customers want and how you can best deal with them. Remember this if you are new to targeting this particular group of customers because there might be times when you feel frustration as a result of not feeling correctly equipped. Interactions will become easier, especially if you are paying attention and working on being comfortable around this group of people. Even if you feel slightly terrified every time you have to pick up the phone and call an ultra-wealthy person to offer your product or services, realize that it will not always be a terrifying experience. As you start to understand what you can expect from your interactions with affluent customers, you will probably begin to feel more confident, and before you know it, these interactions will feel second nature.

Recognize flaws

What should you do if you continue to deal with affluent customers on a daily basis, yet you never seem to be at ease with these interactions? What if you never figure out how to predict your customers' behavior patterns, and as a result, you are unable to offer what the customers really want or need? After all, not all businesses thrive, and there is no way to guarantee that your business will become wildly successful when marketing and selling to affluent customers. How do you get over slumps and start leading your business toward success?

Steer clear of lines of thinking that lead you down the path of trying to analyze what is wrong with your customers. Far too many business owners place the blame squarely on the shoulders of their customer base and assume the customers simply have not yet realized what a great product or service is being offered. Although it might be the case that prospective customers are not aware of your product or service, this does not mean the blame falls on them. Instead, look toward your marketing efforts to figure out why this customer base is unaware of how great your product or service is. It is not the population's fault it is unaware of your product or service; it is your fault. This is when you need to step back and take a look at your marketing efforts and maybe even revise your marketing plan. This is one of the reasons why it is so important to have a marketing plan in place; if it does not work, you have a written record of specific marketing tactics that should not be used anymore because of their ineffectiveness.

You have a different scenario on your hands if you receive plenty of interest from affluent customers initially, but then they fail to make the final purchase. This tells you that you do indeed have a product wealthy people are interested in, but either the product is being offered at too steep a price or something is wrong with the way you present yourself. This is not to say something is fundamentally wrong with you as a person, but instead it points to a need for you to hone your skills as a salesperson when dealing with this specific group. It can certainly be a fine line between enthusiasm and downright giddiness, friendliness and a too-casual demeanor, and being detail-oriented compared to being controlling.

Do not panic if you come to the conclusion you need to overhaul your own behavior in order to help your business succeed. You do not have to fundamentally change who you are, but you probably do need to make some changes to how you handle yourself in business interactions. Think of this less as a change of personality and more of an enhancement of business behavior.

Some salespeople make the mistake of considering their personality at work to be concrete and a direct representation of who they fundamentally are. Ask these salespeople to change their behavior, and there is a good chance that they will be highly insulted. Do not fall into this trap of thinking you are who you are, and there is no way to change your behavior because that would be "selling out." If you need to change the way you present yourself, it does not change who you are as a person. Instead, it is a strategic move to help your business grow. Remember that you are presenting a product to potential customers, and you are a part of that product. Affluent customers want to like and trust the people they purchase goods and products from, so present yourself as likeable and trustworthy in all interactions with these customers. You are not "faking it;" you are simply giving your customers what they need to be comfortable with making a purchase. Think of it as though you are an actor playing a role; you play the part of a successful salesperson, and then when it is all said and done and the transaction is complete, you can go back to being whoever you want to be.

Ask people close to you to give you a frank analysis of your personality. Are you overbearing? Do you intimidate people? Does it seem as though you are not listening to people? If you promise the people close to you that you will not get offended by their criticisms, you might be surprised at what you can discover. You might have personality attributes you never realized you had. Also, be sure to keep up your end of the bargain and by not becoming offended or reacting defensively to your friends and family when they help you with this analysis. You do not want to scare them off from making observations like this in the future. So instead of leaving the conversation in an angry huff when you are told by a loved one that you often convey an air of conceit, ask more questions and thank your loved one for helping you. Observations such as these can help you hone your people skills, which ultimately will result in helping you to better deal with your affluent customer base.

Alternatively, if your product or service is not selling as it should, do not immediately jump to the conclusion that the real problem is you and your behavior when dealing with your customers. It might be that there is simply not a need or want for what you offer, or it might be that the product you offer is not the best option available. Be sure to look at your evaluations from every angle, and exhaust every opportunity to improve the product or service you offer along with the way you personally offer the product or service. Remember to evaluate the way anyone working on your behalf conducts business, as well. It might be true that you have a fantastic product and that you are quite adept at dealing with your customers, but what if your employees are not delivering the type of customer service you expect them to deliver? It might be that your customers walk into your shop ready to make a purchase only to be dissuaded from doing so because your staff is busy having a rowdy conversation about last night's party. If this is the case, you obviously need to take immediate action to ensure careless employees do not further damage your business.

About Your Customers

Consider hiring a mystery-shopping company to help you evaluate the customer service your employees offer. For a fee, one of these shoppers will go into your place of business or call one of your representatives and pose as a customer. Later, they will submit a full report of what the experience was like.

Prepare for changes

As your customer base strengthens, your marketing strategies will undoubtedly change. You will realize which tactics are effective and which tactics simply do not work. Do not think that a marketing strategy that works beautifully at first will always work so well; as times change so do the ways that customers react to marketing.

Consider the spending habits of the wealthy during the worst parts of the Great Recession. Even many of the customers who could afford to keep spending with reckless abandon scaled back, presumably as a show of sensitivity and camaraderie with the people who were affected by the economy. Many of those who did not scale back on their spending wanted to make it less obvious that they were making purchases. They opted to have purchases delivered to their homes instead of walking out of an extravagant store with numerous bags brimming with purchases. If your marketing strategy prior to the recession was to emphasize how expensive and luxurious the items you sold were, this tactic might have worked wonderfully until the economic climate experienced a huge downturn. If you had continued with the same marketing tactic despite that customers were starting to ask for plain paper bags instead of bags featuring your store logo, your inattention to detail would have cost you many customers. Shoppers who already felt guilty about making extravagant purchases might have become uncomfortable visiting your store.

Likewise, you might find yourself needing to change the products you offer. The items that are must-haves this year might become jokes next year, and you need to be keenly in tune with these changes. Many trends start with the affluent and then trickle down the economic ladder, so you can expect your customers to be aware of the upcoming trends. If you sell cars, know about the new safety features slated to be unveiled two years from now. If you sell clothing, know what the designers are presenting and what trends fashion experts predict. If you own a house cleaning business, research the latest ideas about sustainable cleaning products. Ideally, you will be able to offer these things to your customers before they even know that they want them. Help your affluent customers become trendsetters and you will increase the odds of them returning to you for more.

Marketing is not About You

Unless you are affluent, you can only try your best to understand what compels affluent people to buy the things they buy. It is simply not enough to decide you like something or react well to a particular marketing tactic and assume everyone else will as well. You also need to stay away from assuming that all affluent people have butlers and eat their dinners on silver platters. Many of today's affluent drive their own cars and cook their own food, but they just happen to have more money than the majority of the population. Do not allow your assumptions and personal preferences to form your marketing strategy. Base your marketing on what has worked in the past and what you can predict with some confidence will work again.

The wrong focus

Your marketing and selling tactics will falter if you rely on broad sweeping generalizations about who affluent people are and what they will spend their money on. Although it is safe to assume most affluent people will fall into certain categories of spending, throwing every single affluent person into this category and fashioning your entire marketing strategy based on these generalizations might cause you trouble in the future.

C ompare the commission a successful real estate agent in a middle-class neighborhood earns compared to the commission earned by a successful real estate agent working in a highly prestigious affluent neighborhood, and it quickly becomes obvious why dealing with an affluent customer base can be incredibly lucrative. A salesperson working in a jewelry store in a typical mall might not even earn commission or might earn a small portion of the sales, which will not amount to anywhere near the impressive commission a salesperson can earn working in an exclusive jewelry store with just one sale in a day. The examples of the payoff of selling and marketing to affluent customers can go on and on, as there are myriad reasons why it can be a lucrative business decision to turn your focus to wealthy customers.

Simply put, affluent customers have the money to spend. There are plenty of additional potential benefits to dealing with this particular customer base, including the trickle-down effect that makes other people want your product or service, but when it comes right down to it, it simply makes sense to try to sell your product or service to the people who can afford it. Impress affluent customers with what you offer, and there is an excellent chance that your business will succeed.

Patience is a Virtue

It typically takes any business time to get off the ground and build up a solid customer base, but it can be even more difficult when trying to appeal to affluent customers. Affluent customers — especially affluent customers who are among the mega-rich — are in the minority of the population, so you will have fewer customers to market and sell your product to. On the other hand, there is a bigger potential for success if you succeed in your efforts. Some salespeople will toil for one sale after another, but a salesperson dealing with expensive items for an affluent customer base might not need to toil quite so much for individual sales but instead have the ability to turn his or her efforts toward occasional sales. This allows the salesperson to take the time to cultivate relationships and truly learn how to fulfill the needs of his or her customers.

It might take time to get your marketing and selling efforts where you want them to be, and it will more than likely take quite a bit of adjusting. The key is to remember that anything worth having is worth working hard for, and this includes a successful business. If you are in the beginning stages of starting your business, or if you know that you need to shoot a heavy dose of enthusiasm into your existing business, keep these five tips in mind:

1. Do something every day that will contribute to your eventual success, whether that is reading a book about sales and marketing success, joining a professional organization, or making some telephone calls to prospective customers.

2. Keep reminding yourself about your own merits and good traits. If you hope to deal with affluent customers, you will have to be sure of yourself on many levels. Confidence is crucial, so do whatever you have to do in order to remain confident.

3. Know your product inside and out. If you own a house cleaning company, join the crew for a couple of days to see what it is actually like to clean a house. If you sell fine chocolates, sample the chocolates to make sure you can speak about them from experience. This will also help you appear more confident because you can speak with authority about the product or service you offer.

4. Put yourself in your customers' shoes. Affluent customers might present a sense of urgency about things you might not necessarily classify as urgent, such as a social event, but keep in mind that for this particular population this is indeed an urgent matter. If your customer says something

is urgent, you better believe it is urgent and give it your attention as a result.

5. Have passion for what you do. If you start to lose passion for your business, you start to wonder whether all of the extra effort in marketing and selling to affluent customers is worth it. Take vacations and time off to help keep your fire fueled because tirelessly working at a constant pace is enough to burn anyone out from any job, whether it's marketing, selling, or anything else.

Know Your Customers

You will soon realize that affluent people are just as varied as all other groups of people. They have the common denominator of having a lot of money among them, but you simply cannot lump all affluent people into one category. Not all wealthy people are aggressive, charitable, extroverted, or savvy with their money. Furthermore, not all affluent people will stay affluent, just like not all people within the lower income brackets will stay there. Get to know your affluent customers as people as opposed to seeing them as rich people who might give you money for something. If you want to have continued success with your business, you have to convey the feeling to your affluent customers that you value them as people and you understand their needs.

The sitcom *Frazier* featured two brothers who were affluent (both characters were psychiatrists) and who displayed many of the same characteristics attributed to wealthy people, albeit in an extreme and comical way. They preferred wine over beer, going to the opera over going to the movies, and gourmet cuisine over the "regular" meals their father enjoyed. In the tenth season of the show during an episode entitled *Door Jam*, Frazier and his brother Niles visit an exclusive spa that is so exclusive it does not advertise its services, discourages word-of-mouth, and is only open to customers who receive a personalized invitation in the mail.

At first, Frazier and Niles are incredibly impressed by the services offered by the spa. They enjoy their massages and fawn over the skin care gift bags they are given at the conclusion of their visit. It is when they notice a high-profile politician using a special card in a swiping machine to walk through a gold door that they realize there is a "Gold Level" that they do not have access to. Suddenly, the services they received that they were just praising do not seem nearly as spectacular. They plot to find a way into the Gold Level despite a friend's warning that after the Gold Level there are probably even more levels, and all of this is nothing more than a marketing ploy to keep them spending money.

The brothers eventually wind up in the Gold Level of the spa and fawn over the services offered there, just as they did with the other services before realizing the level structure. It is while they are enjoying the amenities of the Gold Level that they realize there is a platinum door, which a spa attendant advises them to stay away from. This enrages them because it makes them believe there is a whole other level of membership they are being kept from. They argue that they are affluent people working in prestigious careers, so there is no reason why they should be kept from what they assume is the Platinum Level.

Of course, the episode takes a comedic turn as they force their way through the platinum door and quickly realize they are now in the back alley near the dumpsters and that this was the reason why the spa attendant asked them to stay away from the door. It was not another level of service from the salon but instead was an exit employees use to dump trash. The episode, while quite funny, does point out an interesting trait many affluent people share; they want to enjoy the best of the best because they feel they deserve it. It is not enough to gain access to the exclusive spa if there is additional exclusivity within the spa itself. Your customers want access to everything you have to offer and might be even more interested if they have the idea that not everyone is entitled to what you offer. They want to feel special and expect to experience things that not everyone is allowed to experience. This is the key to marketing and selling to affluent customers.

Success now ... and Later

Your success in dealing with affluent customers is not just about this moment in time. If you successfully market and sell to this particular customer base, you are carving out a piece of future success for the product you offer. Many products have become household names thanks to the successful marketing and sales efforts that solely targeted wealthy customers, and though some of these products remained specific to affluent customers and others experienced a trickle-down effect that resulting in infiltration into the middle class and beyond, many of these products experienced success that even surprised the products' developers. Nearly everyone knows what a Bentley is, largely thanks to the Hip Hop community that embraced this luxury vehicle. On the other hand, few people outside of the auto aficionados within the affluent population would recognize a Bugatti Veyron if it came rolling down the street. It might take a little longer to get your product or service to a point to where affluent customers want to open their wallets, but once you get to that point, the obvious benefits are numerous.

Always think long term when marketing and selling to affluent customers. You do not want to aim to only make customers happy the moment they are dealing with you, but instead aim to make them happy for much longer. You want your product or service to be the one that naturally comes to mind when affluent customers want to make a purchase.

Do not underestimate your affluent customers. Slick marketing tactics and disingenuous salespeople will not lead you to success. You have to convey the truth about your product while also believing in the product wholeheartedly, and you have to treat affluent customers with a great deal of respect. After all, these are the customers who will propel you into a successful business, and as such, they certainly deserve your respect.

Bibliography

5 Social Media Risks for Companies and Employees...
And How to Prevent Them. *Social Times*. Retrieved from
www.socialtimes.com/2010/06/5-social-media-risks-for-companies-and-employees-and-how-to-prevent-them.

About Face; Physiognomy and Economics. (2009, March 7).
The Economist.

Business: Bling is back; Luxury goods. (2010, October).
The Economist, 397(8705), 81. Retrieved October 27, 2010,
from ABI/INFORM Global. (Document ID: 2171511341).

Friedman, B. D. (2009). Members only: Elite clubs and the
process of exclusion. *International Social Science Review*, 84(3),
187. Retrieved from **http://search.proquest.com/docview/227345110?accountid=13787.**

Making the Most of Wired Society; Social Media Offer Cheap,
Effective Marketing. *Ottawa Citizen*. (2010, October).

Oechsli, M. (2010). Psychografics: profiling the affluent mind. *Registered Rep*, 34(9), 90. (September).

Oeschsli, M. (2005). *The Art of Selling to the Affluent: How to Attract, Service, and Retain Wealthy Customers & Clients for Life.* Hoboken, New Jersey: John Wiley & Sons, Inc.

Pisani, Joseph. (2010). Medical Professionals Still Among Highest Paid in America. CNBC, Friday, 14 May 2010. Retrieved from **www.cnbc.com/id/30644766/Highest_Paying_Jobs_2010?slide=1**.

Rebecca Penty. (2010).That which makes an entrepreneur tick; Traits Venture capitalist and TV personality shares the secrets of success. *Telegraph-Journal*, B.1. (October 29). Retrieved October 31, 2010 from Canadian Newsstand Complete. (Document ID: 2175013761).

RetailMeNot.com; Coupons Are the New Normal. *Computers, Networks & Communications*, 243. (2010, October). Retrieved October 27, 2010 from ProQuest Computing. (Document ID: 2161350391).

Russell, June. (2006). Attractiveness and Income for Men and Women in Management. Journal of Applied Social Phychology, 21(13), 1039-1057. Retrieved from **http://onlinelibrary.wiley.com/doi/10.1111/j.1559-1816.1991.tb00458.x/abstract**.

Signaling Status with Luxury Goods: The Role of Brand Prominence. (2010, December 6). Retrieved October 27, 2010 from ReportLinker.

Subliminal Advertising – It Works. (2009, October 5). *The Main Report Business Letter*. Retrieved October 27, 2010 from Research Library.

Ueda, Dwight. The Importance of Your Company's Sales Compensation Program. Salary.com. Retrieved from **www.salary.com/Articles/ArticleDetail.asp?part=par394.**

US Patent Issued to EMC on Oct. 19 for "Method for Scoring Customer Loyalty and Satisfaction" (Massachusetts Inventors). (2010, October 20). US Fed News Service, Including US State News. Retrieved October 27, 2010 from Research Library. (Document ID: 2170587531).

Ward, David. (2010). Affluent Gravitating Toward Digital Media, New Ipsos Mendelsohn Survey Finds. ClickZ. September 15, 2010. Retrieved from **www.clickz.com/clickz/ news/1733354/affluent-gravitating-toward-digital-media-new- ipsos-mendelsohn-survey-finds**.

Author Biography

Tamsen Butler is the author of *The Complete Guide to Personal Finance: For Teenagers and College Students*, which won first place in the Young Adult Non-Fiction category of the 2010 Next Generation Indie Book Awards. In addition to the other books she has written, Tamsen writes for a few of her local publications, including *The Regency Review* and *Momaha Magazine*. She also writes for a variety of websites, including LoveToKnow and BabiesOnline. She has two vibrant children and stays busy with graduate school, writing, and volunteer work.

Index